# COMPUTER LITERACY SKILLS IN PRACTICE

Students' Book

Graham Bishop,
*Barking College of Technology*

*and*

Fred Caswell,
*Coventry (Lanchester) Polytechnic*

Cartoons drawn by
Elizabeth Gill



McGRAW-HILL Book Company (UK) Limited

**London** · New York · St Louis · San Francisco · Auckland
Bogotá · Guatemala · Hamburg · Johannesburg · Lisbon · Madrid
Mexico · Montreal · New Delhi · Panama · Paris · San Juan
São Paulo · Singapore · Sydney · Tokyo · Toronto

Published by
McGRAW-HILL Book Company (UK) Limited
MAIDENHEAD · BERKSHIRE · ENGLAND

**British Library Cataloguing in Publication Data**

Caswell, Fred
Computer literacy skills in practice.
1. Electronic digital computers
I. Title II. Bishop, Graham,
004 QA76.5

ISBN 0-07-084889-0 Students' bk.
ISBN 0-07-084891-2 Teacher's manual with 40-track disk
ISBN 0-07-084894-7 Teacher's manual with 80-track disk



12345 WL 8987

Typeset by Oxprint Ltd, Oxford, and
printed and bound in Great Britain by Whitstable Litho Limited, Whitstable, Kent

# CONTENTS

# PREFACE

It is becoming increasingly important these days for those entering or already in employment to have some knowledge of computers. This fact has been recognized by the inclusion of a computer literacy module in the Youth Training Scheme. It is towards that scheme that this book is primarily directed.

The aim of this book is to give a general introduction to the world of computers. It is directed at those who have little knowledge of computers, but feel that they would like, or need, more. It attempts to explain the jargon and terminology of computers in simple terms. The author has called upon his long experience in computers and education to present the language of the computer specialist in simple terms.

Starting from a general view of the need for computer literacy and a description of what a computer is, this book moves on to look at the component parts of the computer. It develops to discuss how a computer is used and what it is used for. The author looks at what computer systems are, and how they are developed. Finally, there is a personal view of the future of computing and some of its possible effects on society.

Although there is some discussion of the way the computer works, detailed explanations are beyond the scope of this book. The emphasis is on elementary explanations for the non-specialist. In all chapters the author has tried to relate the material to everyday situations that the non-specialist can identify and understand.

While this book is directed at the Youth Training Scheme, it should also appeal to anybody who wants or needs to know more about computers. It will be suitable for parents whose children are learning about computers at school, for those who are coming into contact with computers at work, or for those who are just curious.

In schools and colleges this book is suitable not only for the Youth Training Schemes, but also for BTEC general level courses, RSA, CPVE, BTEC national level business studies courses, and GCSE and A level courses in computer studies.

The assignments and programs mentioned in this text can be found in the accompanying teacher's manual. It is hoped that students using this book will work through the assignments and programs as they cover the text.

Finally, the author would like to acknowledge the work of Graham Bishop in preparing the *Teacher's Manual*, Nicola Roden for her help in typing the manuscript, Liz Gill for some excellent cartoons, and to Pegasus Software and Midland Bank plc for use of some of their material. Thanks are also due to Anthea Coombs of McGraw-Hill for her advice, but mostly for her patience.

*FC*

Cashpoint

## CHAPTER 1

# What is Computer Literacy?

## WHY YOU NEED TO BE A COMPUTER LITERATE

You cannot go very far these days without encountering a computer. It has become an essential aid to modern business. Very often you will not realize that a computer is involved, even though you can see that a new method is being used for an old job. For example, you may go into a major store and find that the assistant does not use a cash register when taking your money, but instead passes something that looks like a small torch, across the stripes/number on a tag that he or she has removed from the article. This torch-like device or 'bar-code reader' actually reads directly to a computer. The computer then finds the price of the article directly from its files and sends it back to be printed on the cash till role. At the same time the computer notes in its files that the sale has been made so that the shop can reorder that article, if necessary, and statistics about sales can be produced for the shop management.

## CASHPOINTS

Outside banks you will see cashpoints where customers can get money without having to wait at a counter, or even when the bank is closed. The cashpoint is connected by a telephone line to the bank's computer. It reads a number from a card which the customer puts into the cashpoint, finds the customer's account details from its files, and decides whether the customer can have the money he or she has requested. The cashpoint is usually many miles from the computer. Because users often need to be connected to a computer that is many miles away, or computers need to be connected to other computers across vast distances, the use of telephone lines has become an essential part of computer technology.

## MICROCOMPUTERS

It is not only in large businesses, however, that you will find computers in use. Over the last few years the cost of a computer has been greatly reduced. Microtechnology has meant that computing power has come within the reach of households as well as businesses. Even very small companies are buying computers and using them to help with their administrative work.

What does this mean for you? It means that you may find that the jobs you do have changed because of the computer. You may find yourself involved with keyboards and display screens where once you would have been involved with forms and books. You may find that a catalogue has been replaced by a magnetic disk, and a computer is needed to look up prices. You may find that a computer has replaced the office typewriter.

## NEW METHODS

Let me give you an example of how the computer has changed a method of doing a job. Not long ago I opened a new savings account at my local branch of a leading building society. This building society has a national computer network. Before this came into operation I would have gone to the branch office, filled in a form, and paid in my money. There would then have been a wait of several days while my form was sent to head office, processed, and a new passbook issued and posted to me.

Now, however, the counter clerk is able to open my account and issue me with a passbook immediately by using a *visual display unit* (VDU) behind the counter which is connected to the head office computer. The clerk keys in my personal details through a keyboard connected to the VDU. This is immediately recorded on the head office computer files, along with the amount of money I have paid in. In return the computer allocates an account number, and prints all the details on a passbook through a small printer which is attached to the VDU. There is no delay, no sending of forms to head office, with the associated risk of them being lost, and I received my new passbook immediately instead of having to wait for some days.

What does this mean for the counter clerk? He now does his job in a different way. Instead of using a paper form he fills in a form on a VDU screen guided by the computer. He more or less talks to the computer. Above all, his actions directly affect the computer files at head office. If he makes a mistake those files may be incorrect and thus his job becomes more important, more responsible.

*Now work on Assignment 1 in the* Teacher's Manual.

## THE MEANING OF COMPUTER LITERACY

When you eventually find a job you may well become involved with computers in some way. The computer has become essential to modern business and industry. There are few areas where it is not used, in shop, office, or factory. It is important that you are computer literate.

But what is meant by being literate? Does it mean knowing exactly how the computer works? I do not think so. You do not need to know how the computer works to be able to use one, in the same way as you do not need to know how a car works to be able to drive one. The computer is a tool. This book will treat it as one. Later chapters will describe in simple terms how parts of the computer do work, but the complexities will be left to the electronics expert.

Do you need to be able to write BASIC programs? Again, I do not think so, although some of you will learn to write BASIC programs, perhaps to a very high standard. You will learn, however, that BASIC is only one programming language, some would say not a very important one. Some would also argue that computer programmers in business and industrial computer departments are a disappearing race. Their skills will not be required in the future because the businessman will buy his programs when he buys his computer. Programmers will only be employed by a few specialist companies that develop the programs that are sold with the computers.

Being able to design and play games on the computer does not mean that you are computer literate. You may learn from playing some computer games. Some can teach you a great deal about the way the computer makes decisions, about the way it stores data, and about the way in which you have to enter data to the computer through a terminal. You will not find, however, the computer being used for playing games in the business world. It is too valuable a tool to be wasted on game playing.

*Now work on Assignment 2 in the* Teacher's Manual.

Being computer literate means understanding how the computer has affected our everyday lives and the jobs we do; it is knowing how this powerful new tool is used, its potential, and its limitations.

Being computer literate means being able to cope with new methods and new equipment. You may find, for example, that the forms you use are designed in a different way. You may even be filling in forms that are displayed on a screen instead of being printed on paper. You could be 'talking' to the computer through the keyboard and receiving replies and instructions from the computer through the display screen. You will need to do you job with more care, because your mistakes could now have far reaching effects.

Talking to the computer

It is not only in your future jobs that you will come into contact with computers. You will meet them in shops, banks, hotels, even your own home. They may cause you annoyance at times. The computer error has become a common excuse for inefficiency. Being computer literate may help you cope better with the computer error, or even overcome the inefficiency.

The computer has caused many new words and terms, what we call 'jargon', to enter our language: words such as software and bytes, terms such as high level languages and real-time systems. To be computer literate you need to know what these new words and terms mean.

## AIM OF THIS BOOK

The aim of this book is to describe the new equipment that you will meet because of the computer and to explain how this equipment has caused new methods to be used. It will also explain the new words and terminology and help you become computer literate.

## CHAPTER 2

# What is a Computer?

## THE PARTS OF A COMPUTER

The computer has been called an electronic brain. This is because it works rather like a brain. It receives an *input* of facts, which computer people call *data*. It organizes this data and *stores* it away for later use. It *outputs* the organized facts as *information* as and when required.

Basically, however, the computer is nothing more than a complex machine. To do the work of a brain it needs:

1. An input device or devices, its ears or eyes. You will probably have seen a *keyboard* as the input device for the computers you have used. There is a wide range of input devices that can be used to input data, as we shall see in Chapter 3.
2. An output device or devices, the computer's mouth. Some computers can actually produce spoken output. In Chapter 4 we will look at how information is output from a computer.
3. A storage device or devices on which data can be stored away for later use. This is usually called *memory*. In Chapter 5 we will look at the way data is stored, and the types of hardware used to store data.
4. A *processor*, which is usually known as the *central processing unit* (CPU). It is in the CPU where data is organized and decisions are made by the computer about what to do with it. Some data may need to be used in complex calculations. Some may be filed away in storage for later use.

   The CPU has some memory of its own, but not enough to store all the data that a business would need to keep to work properly. Not only that, the data stored here is usually lost when the computer is switched off. This is why other storage devices are needed.

   The memory within the CPU is known as *internal* storage, and the memory available on the other storage devices as *external* or *backing* storage.

The CPU is often regarded as the most important part of the computer. The input, output, and storage devices are referred to as *peripherals*, or *peripheral devices*. Peripheral means on the boundary, so in the case of the computer it means outside the CPU. Some people think that peripheral means extra, and that the peripheral devices are not important. This is not so. The computer cannot work without being able to input data, store data, and output information. We will see in later chapters that when you are designing computer systems, the consideration of how data will be input and stored and of how information will be output is often as important as the consideration of how data will be processed.

To sum up, then, a computer consists of input devices, storage devices, output devices, and a CPU (see Fig. 2.1).

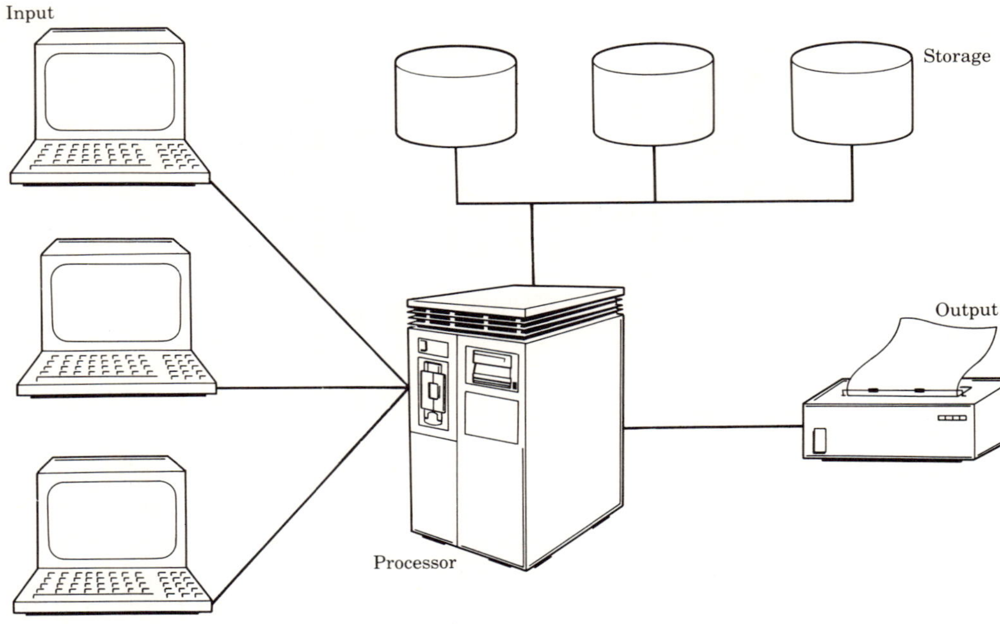


**Figure 2.1** *Parts of a computer*

*Now work on Assignment 3 in the* Teacher's Manual.

## COMPUTER HARDWARE, MICROCOMPUTERS

The machinery of the computer is known as *hardware*. The combination of CPU and peripheral devices that make up a particular computer are often referred to as a *configuration*. Computer configurations vary enormously in size. At one end of the scale the smallest microcomputer will have a CPU no bigger than a cigar box. The only input device will be a keyboard that is part of the CPU. It will need to be plugged into a television set to provide an output device. It will rely upon an ordinary tape cassette deck for its external storage.

At the other end of the scale a mainframe computer will have a large and complex CPU. It will have many external storage devices. It will have a large number of input and output devices of different types, some of which may be vast distances from the computer connected to it by telephone lines. It will be so complex that it will use smaller computers as input and output devices.

In between there is an immense range of computer configurations. The largest microcomputer will be very different from the smallest, having a large CPU and several input, output, and storage devices.

## MINICOMPUTERS

Above the array of microcomputers are the minicomputers, but it is often difficult to distinguish between micros and minis at the point where the two ranges meet.

In the same way, at the top of the minicomputer range minis are every bit as powerful, and handle as many peripheral devices, as small mainframe computers. Large minicomputers are referred to as *super minis*.

## MAINFRAME COMPUTERS

Large mainframe computer configurations may have several mainframes,

A small computer and a large computer

minis, and micros linked together in a huge network. The micros may only be *intelligent terminals* (see Chapter 3) to the mainframes.

The world of computers is very confusing. For your purposes, however, you can consider the microcomputer as being a small configuration usually housed in various parts of a building wherever there is need for one. The minicomputer is a medium-size configuration, slower and less powerful than the mainframe. The mainframe is a large configuration, and very powerful. The minicomputer and mainframe usually require their own special room, often air-conditioned, and trained computer staff to operate them.

## COMPUTER SOFTWARE

The computer is quite different from other machines. Other machines are operated and controlled by a human operator. Think about the way you would use a calculator to multiply together two numbers. First you must press the keys to put the first number into the calculator. Next you press the multiply key. Then you press the keys for the second number. Finally, you press the equals key to show the result in the display window. You have to direct the actions of the machine as it works.

The computer does not work like this. The computer has a CPU. This CPU contains a certain amount of memory. When the computer does a job the set of instructions which tells it every step of the task is stored in the CPU's memory. This set of instructions is known as a *program*. It is this capability, of storing its own instructions, that sets the computer apart from other machines. It means, of course, that before the computer can do any job somebody must sit down and decide exactly how that job is done. Somebody must painstakingly write out, in precise detail, and in the right sequence, every step that must be taken to accomplish the task.

*Now work on Assignments 4 and 5 in the* Teacher's Manual.

Let us return to the task of multiplying two numbers using a calculator. The instructions to do that job are:

1. Input first number.
2. Input second number.
3. Multiply first number by second.
4. Display result.

This is a program, even though it is a very simple one. A computer programmer would write these instructions in an appropriate *programming language* for the computer that is being used (see Chapter 9). It would then be fed into the computer to be stored in the CPU so that the computer knows exactly what steps to take when multiplying two numbers together.

The computer, however, cannot work without a program or programs that tell it exactly what to do. The programs that enable the computer to go about its complex tasks are known as *software*. You can switch on a computer, and press buttons, but without software, the hardware is nothing but an inactive piece of machinery. We can see then, that the computer needs software to be a complete, working machine. It needs a great deal of software. It needs different types of software.

## APPLICATION PROGRAMS

People and organizations buy computers because they want particular jobs done. They sit down and write the programs to do those jobs. The buyer of a home computer may write programs to play games, or to keep an account of the food in a deep freeze, and so help the family budget.

A business may write programs to keep stock records or produce employees' pay slips. They are written for a particular job or application. These sort of programs are known as *application programs*.

## APPLICATION PACKAGES

Some people or organizations choose to save the task of sitting down and writing programs for someone else. A business may not want to employ skilled programming staff. They tend to be expensive. A business may also find that it sometimes requires software that is complex and the writing of it is beyond the skill of its own programmers. In such cases the answer may be to buy the required programs from organizations that specialize in writing software for particular jobs, ready packed. You can see why these programs are known as *application packages*.

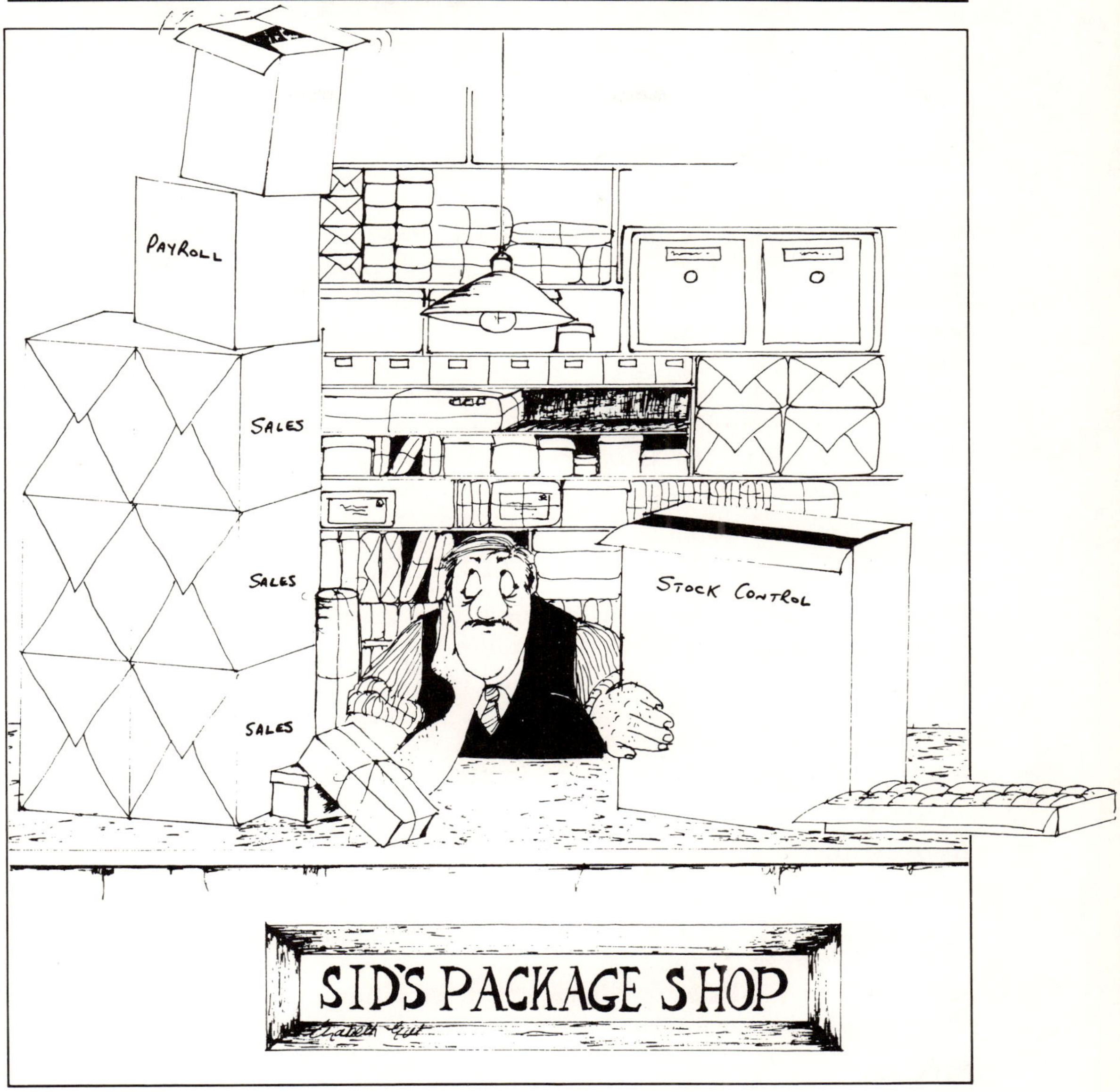


Package shop

## UTILITY PROGRAMS

There are some jobs that the computer is called upon to do over and over again, no matter who the user is. For example, data must often be copied from one storage device to another. It is important to keep copies of data, in the same way as it is important to keep copies of letters or other documents. Similarly, data on storage devices often needs to be sorted into particular sequences. Computer programs to carry out these tasks are in fairly regular demand. As these programs are relatively simple, and work in much the same way, there is little point in every computer user sitting down to write these programs over and over again. As a result they are usually provided by the computer manufacturers or sellers. Such programs are known as *utility programs*.

## TRANSLATORS

In an attempt to simplify the task of programming, computer programmers write their programs in languages more readily understandable to themselves rather than to the computer. As a result, software is needed to translate the programs into a form that the computer can understand. These programs are known as *compilers*, *assemblers*, or *interpreters*. You will learn more about them in Chapter 9.

## OPERATING SYSTEMS

There is one more type of software that is essential to the modern computer. It involves very complex software. Without it most computers could not do anything. This software is needed in order to get application programs, packages, utilities, compilers, or assemblers into the CPU. This software controls the running of the computer. It makes sure that unauthorized people cannot use the computer or get their hands on data and programs. It ensures, on mini and mainframe computers, that the large number of input and output devices all get their fair share of the computer. This software is the *operating system*. We will not look at this type of software in detail because it is beyond the scope of this book.

## THE ADVANTAGES OF COMPUTERS

Finally, in this chapter let us consider why the computer has become such a vital, indispensable tool for the modern business organization.

### *Speed*

The computer is fast. It can perform a vast number of calculations in a fraction of a second. It can do in minutes jobs that once took an army of clerks hours.

### *Repetition*

The computer does not mind boring, repetitive work. It will gladly do the same monotonous task over and over again, without tiring, and without making mistakes. When you consider these two points, you can see why the computer is likely to mean a great reduction in the number of people the businessman needs to employ.

### *Storage*

The computer can store on its storage devices enormous amounts of data in a very small space. It can also find that data very quickly when required. It is not uncommon for computers in England to find data kept on storage devices in America.

### *Accuracy*

The computer is accurate. Once it has been correctly programmed to do a job, it will do that job correctly every time. It is people who make mistakes, not computers. The businessman, therefore, has better control of his business.

*Now work on Assignment 8 in the* Teacher's Manual, *and on Programs A and B on the disk.*

## CHAPTER 3

# Data Capture

### WHY DATA CAPTURE?

We now know what a computer is and what we mean by computer systems. The next areas to consider are the different parts of a computer and the way they are used.

You may wonder why this chapter is called 'Data Capture'. It is because we must always be sure that all the data that a computer system needs gets into the system and that none of it gets lost or escapes. You can see why, with words like 'lost' and 'escape', we refer to data capture. In this chapter we will be looking at the ways in which we can ensure that the data we enter into the computer through its various input devices has in fact been entered correctly.

Capturing data

## KEYBOARD DATA CAPTURE

Most of you will have only seen computer systems where data is input directly through a keyboard. The data is displayed on a screen as it is entered. On microcomputers it is usually the only way to input data, but many large computer systems also use this method of data capture. You can see for yourselves, in banks, building societies, travel agencies, and other such places, how much VDUs are used for inputting data. The people who operate VDUs enter data as soon as a customer makes a transaction, such as paying in money or booking a holiday. The data is written into the computer's storage immediately. This is known as *on-line* data capture, because the person entering the data is connected directly to the computer, or on-line to it. It is also sometimes called data capture at source. The data enters the system at the source of the transaction.

Data entered in this way is often done by staff who are neither computer experts nor expert typists. They often do other jobs as well as entering data through a VDU keyboard. Sometimes they are many miles from the computer, connected to it by a telephone line. They will be slow at entering data. You will know yourselves, if you have tried typing in data on your micro, how slow it is.

## MAN–MACHINE DIALOGUES

Non-expert typists are liable to make many mistakes entering data. Human beings are not very good at doing this sort of work. The people who design computer systems, therefore, have to take great care to make sure that the system is easy for the keyboard operator to use, and that it is difficult to make mistakes when entering data. We usually say that the system must be *user friendly*. These designers have to develop a way for the system to 'talk' to the operator and tell the operator what to do. It is known as a dialogue, a *man–machine dialogue*. The operator is given instructions on the VDU screen, and replies to the system through the keyboard. The operator enters data into the system in the way the system tells him to do so. Let us look at two ways in which the system can talk to the operator: by *menu selection* and *form filling*.

### *Menu selection*

Menu selection means that the operator is given a list of options on the display screen from which to choose the entry required. It is like choosing things from a menu in a cafe. For example, suppose a person is entering data on a payroll system, telling the computer about changes to the workers on the payroll. The operator can enter data about new workers joining the payroll, workers leaving the payroll, or change the details of workers already on the payroll. A display would then appear on the screen that looks like this:

Changes to payroll
1. Add new worker.
2. Remove old worker.
3. Change worker's details.
Select the option you require

The operator enters the correct number according to what has to be done.

Figure 3.1 shows a menu from a well-known software package. Entering data in this way is very easy for the operator. There is nothing to remember. It is only necessary to press a few keys. It is difficult to make mistakes.

«« PEGASUS »» Sales Ledger 29 Mar 8-

Pegasus Software

1. A/c Name & Address Update
2. Ledger Postings
3. List Invoices & C/Notes
4. List Receipts & Adjustments
5. Enquiries
6. Statements
7. Aged Debtors List
8. List of Accounts
9. Outstanding Debtors Total
0. Terminate

Select Function & Press Appropriate Number

**Figure 3.1** *Menu*

### *Form filling*

Form filling means that the operator sees displayed on the screen a form, just like a paper form. The form is filled in by moving the cursor to the boxes to be completed and typing in the data needed. It is not much different from filling in a paper form, so it is easy for the operator.

PLEASE CHECK ENTRY

EMPLOYEE NAME — TAX RATE 30. %

J.SMITH ESQ — N.I. RATE 12 %

WEEKLY PAY £ 100.00 — SUPER.RATE 6. %

| WEEK NO. | PAY/WEEK | ADJ TO PAY +/- | GROSS PAY | TOT. PAY TO DATE | DEDUCTIONS TAX +/- | NI | SUP | TAX TO DATE | NET PAY |
|---|---|---|---|---|---|---|---|---|---|
| 1 | 100 | -18 | 82 | 82 | 24 | 9 | 4 | 24 | 45 |
| 2 | 100 | -16 | 84 | 166 | 25 | 10 | 5 | 49 | 44 |
| 3 | 100 | 3 | 103 | 269 | 30 | 12 | 6 | 79 | 55 |
| 4 | 100 | 3 | 103 | 372 | 30 | 12 | 6 | 109 | 55 |
| 5 | 100 | -15 | 85 | 457 | 25 | 10 | 5 | 134 | 45 |
| 6 | 100 | -8 | 92 | 549 | 27 | 11 | 5 | 161 | 49 |
| 7 | 100 | 16 | 116 | 665 | 34 | 13 | 6 | 195 | 63 |

H L E N

**Figure 3.2** *Payroll*

The operator working on our payroll system might use a form like the one shown in Fig. 3.2 for entering details of a new worker to be put on the payroll.

Figure 3.3 shows a screen form from a well-known software package.

## DATA VALIDATION

You will see that at the top of the form for the entry of the payroll details (Fig. 3.2) there is an instruction for the operator to check that the data has been entered correctly. We have already seen that operators are liable to make many errors entering data. We must do all we can to stop wrong data from getting into our computer systems. You may have heard the saying

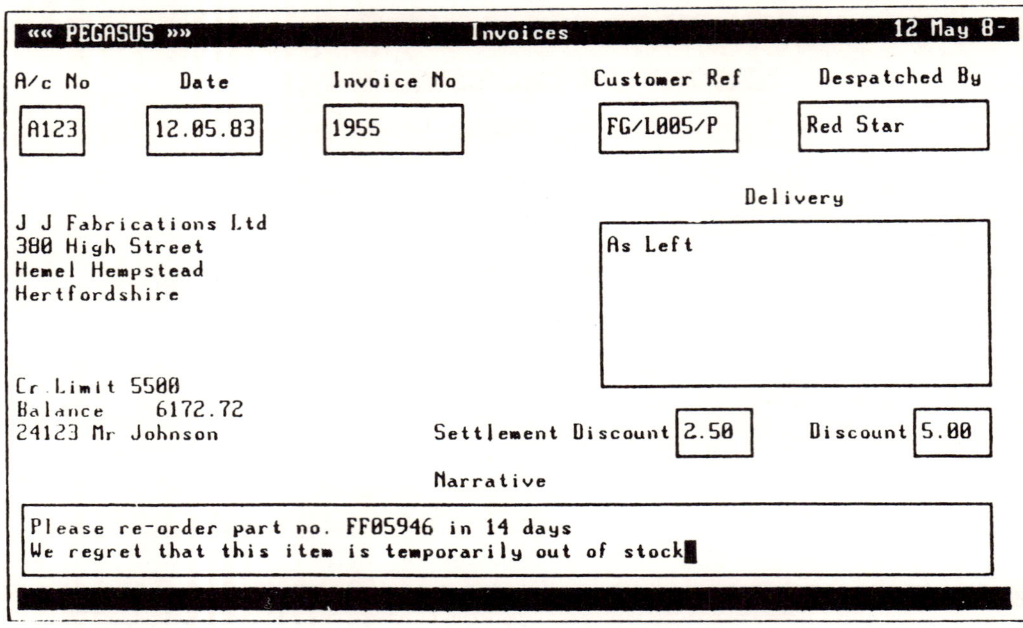


**Figure 3.3** *Invoice*

'garbage in—garbage out'. It means that if we put rubbish into our computer systems we will get rubbish out. Asking operators to check their entries is one way of stopping rubbish getting into the system.

*Now work on Assignment 9 in the* Teacher's Manual.

No matter how well operators check their entries, mistakes will be made in entering data. To try and find these mistakes we can ask the computer to look at the data as it enters the system to see if it looks correct. This means that the computer program will have to look at each data item and make sure that it meets certain rules. This is known as *data validation*. There are several types of check that can be made on data items.

### *Format checks*

Format checks make sure that the data item is of the right type; for example, if a data item should only have numbers in it, the computer will complain if letters are entered.

### *Range checks*

Range checks make sure that the data item falls within acceptable limits; for example, if a worker should never work more than 60 hours per week, the computer will complain if an operator enters more than 60 hours in that box.

These checks are easy to program and are simple steps to take to guard against incorrect data capture. Think about how you would make checks to see that a date entered in the format ddmmyy (e.g., 040139 = 4th January 1939) is valid.

### *Check digits*

Another check that can be made on numbers being entered to help prove that it is correct is a *check digit* test. This is a little more difficult than range or format checks. A check digit is an extra digit added to the end of a number. This digit is worked out by doing arithmetic on the number.

This may be difficult to understand, but an example should help make it clear.

We will use a payroll system for our example. Suppose one of the data items that has to be entered is a five digit worker's number. To guard against wrong entry of the number we could add a check digit to it. This can be used to check that the number is entered to the computer system correctly.

Consider a worker's number of 55454. This is a difficult number. Try saying it quickly. It would be very easy to write down this number, or enter it at a keyboard, incorrectly, as 55545, for example. Changing the sequence of the digits in a number, particularly a difficult one like 55454, is a very common mistake. A check digit guards against this.

This is one way of calculating a check digit:

Step 1 Multiply the right hand end digit of the number by two, the next to the left by three, the next to the left by four, and so on, like this:

$4 \times 2 = 8$
$5 \times 3 = 15$
$4 \times 4 = 16$
$5 \times 5 = 25$
$5 \times 6 = 30$

Step 2 Add up the results you get, like this:

$8 + 15 + 16 + 25 + 30 = 94$

Step 3 Divide that total by eleven, like this:

$94 \div 11 = 8$, remainder 6

Step 4 Subtract the remainder from eleven, like this: $11 - 6 = 5$, which is the check digit.

The worker's number now becomes 554545, and this is the six digit number that will always be used for the worker when it is entered to the computer system. This method of calculating a check digit is called *modulus eleven* because we divided by eleven.

You may well wonder why we would do such a strange thing. The answer is simple. Suppose an operator entered the number incorrectly, as 555454. The computer would do exactly the same arithmetic on the first five digits of the number. Do it for yourselves and see what you get. You will get a check digit of two. It should be five, so the computer knows that the number entered is wrong.

Data validation checks are very important. We must be as sure as we can that data gets into our computer systems correctly, or else we will be sending old age pensioners £1 000 000 gas bills.

## DIRECT DIALOGUE

Some systems allow the operator more freedom when entering data and receiving information from the system. These are systems where the operator is more likely to issue orders than enter data. For example, an operator working on an airline booking system will often be asking the system to provide details of flights and will use a different dialogue. It is often known as *direct dialogue*. The following might be the way flight information would be requested:

F:LON:GEN:23/04/85

This is a command to the system. The F means that flight information is needed, LON means flights from London, GEN means flights to Geneva, and the date the flight is needed is 23 April 1985. The computer system will be programmed to understand such commands. The first letter will always indicate the type of command, and the system will always expect to receive next the start point of the flight, followed by the finishing point, then the date. Commands will always be expected in a set way, and will be rejected unless they are typed in that way.

You can see that the operator needs to know more about the system when using such a dialogue. It is necessary to remember how to type in the commands correctly. An operator will probably make more mistakes when using such a system. These sorts of dialogue are usually employed by people who use the computer a great deal in their jobs and who therefore get used to the dialogue. You may already know how to use a dialogue like this. It is the way you issue commands to microcomputer systems.

## IMPROVING INPUT

So far, we have looked at how we capture data for a computer system through a keyboard on a VDU. We have talked about the fact that it is a slow way of entering data and that keyboard operators are liable to make mistakes. The makers of computers have tried to improve the speed at which data can be captured, and to improve the accuracy of data capture, by developing new data capture hardware. Again, you can see examples of this hardware around, particularly in shops. It will become more and more common over the years.

Most of this new hardware cuts down the amount of key pressing that people inputting data have to do. Remember, I said that humans are not very good at that type of thing, so if the amount of key pressing can be cut down there is less chance of mistakes being made when capturing data. We will look at some of this type of hardware, but we do not have enough room in this book to describe all that there is. Look for yourselves when you are out and about to see the sort of hardware there is and how it works.

## BAR-CODE READERS

Most goods that you buy these days have a bar-code printed on them (as shown in Fig. 3.4). They are put there by the companies that make the goods. Bar-codes can be read by light pens or laser readers that are passed

9 780077 070014

**Figure 3.4** *Bar- code*

across the code and measure the width of the bars and the spaces between them. The data read is written directly to the computer's storage. Because the data is captured so quickly it means that shopkeepers can keep much better account of sales and stocks. They should be able to keep more goods on their shelves and, therefore, sell more. At the time the data is read, the prices of the goods are found by the computer, so there is no need to put the price of the goods on each package. Shopkeepers can save staff, or put them to better use.

Some light pens can read printed numbers rather than bar-codes. You will see these in some shops.

## COMPUTER LINKED CASH REGISTERS

Computer linked cash registers are used in many shops. The goods in these shops again do not have prices on them. Instead there is a number printed on the goods' labels. The cash register operator keys in this number when somebody buys an article and the price is found by the computer. The shopkeeper again has all the advantages that are gained by using bar-code readers. The amount of key pressing that has to be done by the operator is greatly reduced.

## BADGE READERS

Badge readers read plastic cards onto which magnetic characters have been written. The cards look like Access™, Barclaycard™, or cheque cards. They are fed into a slot on the front of the badge reader, and the data written on them is read into the computer. Badge readers can be built into cash registers and other such devices. They save the operator having to key in vital data, such as the operator's reference number.

You can all see a badge reader quite easily. Most banks have one on their walls, because cash points are badge readers. Try to see one working. You will also see that a cash point has a special VDU. The keyboard has just a few special keys. It has been designed especially for cash points. Many companies have special keyboards made for their own computer systems these days.

## PASSBOOK READERS

A passbook reader is really a sort of badge reader and, like a VDU, is also an output machine as well as an input machine. It is used in building societies and other companies where people save money or make regular payments that have to be recorded in a book as well as in the computer. The passbook has a magnetic strip in it where the customer's account number is written. It is placed in a slot in the passbook reader. The computer reads the magnetic strip and finds the customer's account from its storage. The operator is saved the job of typing in the account number, so there is no danger of posting money to the wrong account.

The passbook reader also prints in the passbook the details of any payments made and the new account balance after each transaction, so the customer's book is always up to date.

These are just some examples of the sort of data capture hardware you will see coming into use in the age of the computer.

## OFF-LINE DATA PREPARATION

After looking at on-line data capture, we now turn to a different data capture problem. I have said that keying in data through a keyboard on a VDU is a slow job. Sometimes there is a vast amount of data to be entered to a computer system, and the data is received by the company on forms or other documents. Computer people call these *source documents*. For example, a large car maker may receive thousands of orders for spare parts through the post every day. A bank has to input to its computer systems a vast number of cheques every day. There is far too much data to be entered

Passbook reader

by operators through VDU keyboards in the way we have looked at so far.

When large amounts of data have to be entered to a computer system from source documents special staff are needed to key in the data quickly. These staff are known as *data preparation staff*. They have been trained to type data very quickly.

The data from source documents is typed by the data preparation staff and is written onto something that the computer can read. Computer people call the items onto which the data is written *input media*.

### *Punched cards*

In the early days of computers the input medium used was nearly always the punched card. A punched card is usually about six inches by three inches in size with 80 columns across it. One character of data can be punched into each column by a machine that cuts small, rectangular holes in the column when the operator presses a key. Punched cards are not used very often now because cards are flimsy, easily spoilt, hard to store, and can only be used to store data once. This makes them expensive for input purposes. Furthermore, a computer reads punched cards slowly compared with reading, say, magnetic tape. The fact that a card only holds a maximum of 80 characters means that a person punching them must wait for a new card to be fed into the punching machine at frequent intervals. This slows down the data preparation process.

### *Punched paper tape*

With punched paper tape, like punched cards, information is represented by a series of holes in the paper tape. Being a continuous strip of paper there is no limitation to the amount of data held.

### *Magnetic input media*

Because of the drawbacks of punched cards or paper tape, new types of input medium were examined. The best medium to use was found to be a magnetic one, such as magnetic tape or disk. These are stronger than punched cards or paper tape. They are not damaged nor lost as easily. They can be used over and over again. They are easy to store and do not take up much room. The computer reads them very quickly and the data preparation job is done fast and efficiently.

Consequently, the makers of computers brought out machines that write data directly onto magnetic tapes or magnetic disks as the data preparation staff press keys. Some machines write the data onto small, 'floppy' disks. Some write the data onto large, 'hard' disks under the control of a computer, where each operator presses keys on a VDU that is connected to the computer. It sounds like on-line data capture, but it is different because the computer is simply writing the data onto a disk and will not treat it as input until later, when all the data has been entered. Systems where data is written directly to magnetic disk are known as *key-to-disk systems*. Sometimes, where the data is written by the computer directly to a large, hard disk it is called *direct data entry*.

## VERIFYING

When data is being written onto an input medium by data preparation staff it is usual for one person to type the data, and then for another to type it all over again. The first time it is typed it is written onto the tape or disk. The second time it is typed the machine checks that the data is correct and allows the operator to put right any mistakes. The second typing is known as *verifying* the data. The machine compares what was typed the first time with what is typed the second time and indicates if anything is different.

By this method, of course, there is the chance of mistakes being made as the data is typed onto the input medium, as well as the risk of mistakes being made as the data is entered onto the source documents. It is again important that the data is validated by a computer program before it is used by the computer system. There is also a risk that source documents may go missing as they move to the data preparation department. To guard against this happening the source documents are often put into batches and totals of the documents in each batch are checked by the computer as the data is validated.

## DOCUMENT INPUT

The fact that data is typed onto some input medium and then verified before it is ready to be read by the computer means that there is a time delay before the computer can use the data. It would be much quicker if the computer could read source documents directly. The makers of computers have, indeed, made some machines that will read source documents.

### *OCR*

*Optical character readers* (OCRs) can read handwritten or typed characters on documents. The characters must, however, be carefully written. They must also be written in particular places on the documents and the machines will only read a few characters. When such a machine is bought the buyer must decide then which characters will need to be read. You can see that the use of optical character readers is limited. They have not been used very much for data capture yet.

### *MICR*

*Magnetic ink character readers* (MICRs) also read source documents. They are used extensively, mostly in banks. The strange characters seen at the bottom of cheques are magnetic ink characters (see Fig. 3.5). Banks have special machines that read these, which means that they can capture the data from cheques for their computer systems very quickly.

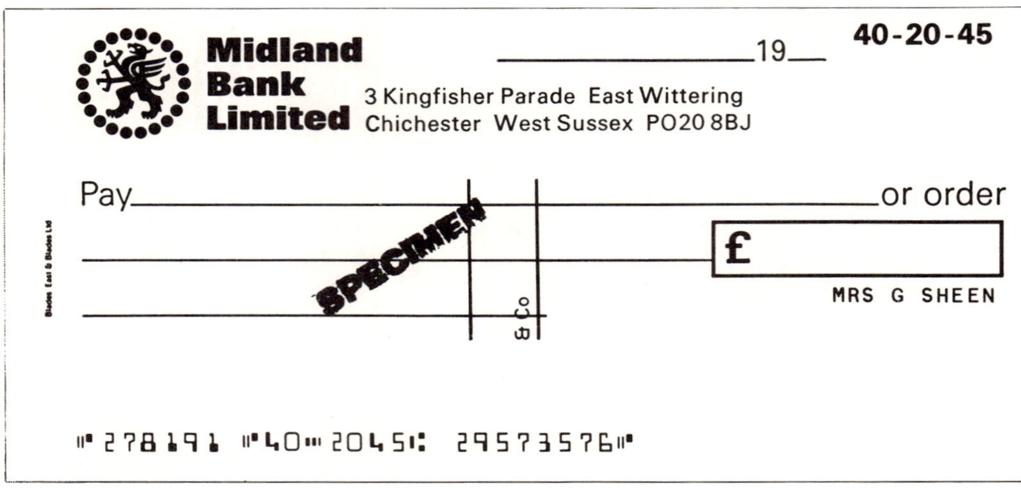


**Figure 3.5** *Cheque with MICR characters*

### *OMR*

Another machine that is used for reading source documents is an *optical mark reader* (OMR). This reads marks, made in ink or pencil, on a form. It knows what data is meant to be read from the position of the mark on the form. Optical mark readers are used for reading data such as answers to multiple choice examination papers, the selection of teams on a football coupon, or meter reading forms.

## FUTURE DEVELOPMENTS

We have given a lot of time to the subject of data capture, because it is a very important aspect of computer systems. The makers of computers are always working on new machines to improve the ways of getting data into our systems. In years to come new ways will be developed. One day we will be able to talk to the computer and it may be able to recognize us and our handwriting. Already there are machines that can recognize fingerprints and signatures.

We must also not forget that many computer systems capture different sorts of data, for example, temperatures from thermometers. There are data capture machines that can measure temperatures, flows of fuel and water, sizes, and weights. This sort of data is needed if we are to use computers to control our cars, factories, and the gadgets we use in the home.

*Now work on the Assignments 10 and 11 in the* Teacher's Manual, *and on Program C on the disk.*

## CHAPTER 4

# Computer Output

## INFORMATION

In the last chapter we looked at the way in which data is captured for our computer systems. We saw how we input data, and the sort of computer hardware that is used for getting data into computer systems. At the other end of the process, we need to get information out. It is no good processing data unless we can see the results of the processing afterwards. In this chapter we will look at the way *information* is *output* from computer systems and the type of hardware that is used.

### *What is information?*

First of all, let us see what is meant by information. It can mean different things to different people. To a person who is using a computer controlled factory system, a flashing light that shows that something is going wrong is information. You may have seen for yourselves that a microcomputer may give information by making bleeping noises to show that something has happened.

Usually, though, we mean characters printed on paper or displayed on a visual display screen when we talk about information. This is the way most people like to see information from computer systems.

Businesses need all sorts of information to operate properly. They need details of stocks of goods and parts to make the goods, details of sales they have made, as well as details of how much they owe their suppliers and how much their customers owe them. Some information must be produced by the business. For example, if a business does not produce bills for its customers it will not be paid any money. If it does not tell the tax people how much money it owes them it will be in considerable trouble. Its workers will not be very happy if they are not shown how much they have earned each week or month.

*Now work on Assignment 12 in the* Teacher's Manual.

## MANAGEMENT INFORMATION

There is some information, however, that does not have to be produced, although the business will not run very well if it is not. This sort of information is known as *management information.* It tells the manager if the business is efficient and making money, or as much money as it should. It will tell the manager about sales and costs and debts and all the other things that should be known to run the businesses properly.

One of the problems with some computer systems is the amount of information they produce. Some printers can print at very high speeds. They can print hundreds of lines each minute. The people who design computer systems are sometimes carried away by the speed with which information

Businessman with huge pile of paper

can be printed. Their computer systems produce so much information that it is impossible to take it all in.

## INFORMATION PRINCIPLES

A computer can be programmed to decide what information should be produced, and when to produce it. Many modern computer systems produce information for managers using certain principles. These are:

1. Information should be produced at the right time, not too late, or even too early.
2. Information should have enough details to allow the person using it to be able to do something about it. For example, if the computer system reports that the business has run out of stock of some vital goods it should also state where to buy some more.
3. Information should be brief, or as brief as possible, with enough details, but not so much that the person receiving it cannot read it in the time

available, or so much that the vital facts are missed. You may have heard the saying 'you can't see the wood for the trees'. This is what the saying means.

4. Finally, but perhaps of most importance, information should be unusual. Managers need to act when they know that something out of the ordinary has happened, usually when something has gone wrong. Many computer systems print lots of information that show that everything is normal. It is much better to get the computer to compare what is happening with past events and to report when something out of the ordinary is going on. For example, the managers of a business might find that they are selling huge quantities of one of their products that normally does not sell very well. They would want to look into this quickly to see why, and to make the most they can out of it. It is this sort of information that computer systems should produce. It might be difficult to see this information easily in a large sales report.

## OUTPUT HARDWARE

Now let us look at the hardware that is used for outputting information from computer systems. Although information can appear as flashing lights, or be heard as warning bleeps or buzzers, usually people want information produced in one of three ways:

1. Displayed.
2. Printed.
3. Drawn.

## DISPLAYED OUTPUT

You will probably be most familiar with displayed information. It is the output method for small computers, especially home computers, where the device used is often the family television. VDUs are like televisions. They can be used to display lines or even parts of a page of characters just like a printer.

There are some display screens that are specially designed to display high definition pictures rather than printed text. They are known as *graphics display units* and are more expensive than normal VDUs. They are used mainly by people who need to display drawn diagrams or figures in their work, people such as builders, designers, or architects.

### *Soft copy*

Computer people call VDUs *soft copy* devices. This is because the information displayed on the screen disappears when it is replaced by other information. To be seen again it has to be recalled to the screen. Unless the information is put away in the computer's storage, or unless it is copied onto a printer, it will be lost for ever. This can cause problems. Many people prefer to have a permanent copy of information.

## PRINTED OUTPUT

Printers give a permanent copy of information. They are called *hard copy* devices by computer people. The information produced on printers can be read over and over again and easily recalled if it is filed properly. There are lots of different types of printer that can be used with computers.

### *Fast printers*

Fast printers usually print a line at a time, although some actually print a whole page at a time. One notable exception to this rule is an ink jet printer, considered to be fast, which prints one character at a time. A range of methods is available to put the print on the page. Some use print chains, some a barrel with the characters that can be printed embossed on the outside of the barrel. Others use laser beams to transfer a photographic image onto the paper.

The printing speed varies from about 300 lines per minute to as much as 12 000 lines per minute. Similarly, the print quality differs from printer to printer. Typically the faster the printer and the better its print quality the more expensive it is. Thus, laser printers give the fastest print speeds and good quality results and accordingly are expensive.

### *Slow printers*

Slow printers print a character at a time. This is the sort of printer likely to be found in use on a microcomputer. Again, a variety of methods is used to put characters on the page.

### *Impact printers*

Some use an impact method, which means that the character being printed actually hits the paper, usually through a ribbon that is soaked with ink. One type of impact printer widely used has a series of needles from which the characters to be printed are formed. They are known as *dot matrix printers*. If you look carefully at characters printed by them you can see that they are made up of a lot of dots.

Other impact printers have sets of characters that hit the paper in the same way that characters are printed by typewriters. Of this type the one generally used is the *daisy wheel printer*. It is called a daisy wheel because it has what looks like a daisy to hold the characters that it can print. The characters are embossed on the ends of spokes that look like the petals of a daisy. The wheel spins round and the characters are hit by a hammer that makes them in turn hit the paper. Daisy wheel printers are more expensive than dot matrix printers, but they give a much better quality print.

There are other types of impact character printers, but the ones we have looked at are the sort most widely used.

### *Non-impact printers*

Non-impact character printers also have several different methods of putting characters on the page. Ink jet printers squirt ink from jets onto the paper. Thermal printers used needles that are hot, and print on a special paper that reacts to the heat. Electrostatic printers work like photocopiers; they put an electric charge onto the paper, and this attracts black plastic particles which are then melted onto the paper. Some character printers work like this, as do laser printers that print a page at a time.

*Now work on Assignments 13 and 14 in the* Teacher's Manual.

## DRAWN OUTPUT

Sometimes drawn output is needed from a computer system. The output devices that are used for drawn output are known as *graph plotters*. They

Daisy wheel

draw pictures, graphs, plans, and other figures by moving pens across paper, or by moving paper across pens. The pens or paper can move in any direction, and different coloured pens are used. The computer is programmed to move the pens or the paper up or down, or backwards or forwards, and to bring selected pens into contact with the paper. In this way figures are drawn. The paper is either fixed flat into a tray, as with the flat bed plotter, or fixed to a revolving drum, as with the drum plotter.

## OTHER OUTPUT METHODS

In this chapter we have looked at the main types of output device used by a computer. There are others that we have not looked at. Computer systems can write information out onto microfilm. Spoken output is possible from some computer systems, and it is likely to become more common in the future. Doubtless new methods will appear over the years.

Computers are also used to control devices such as robots. This is a special type of output that causes things to move the way the computer directs them. The use of computer controlled machinery has become very important in some factories. You may have seen television adverts about cars built by robots.

## OUTPUT TO MAGNETIC MEDIA

We must also remember that data and information are written onto the computer's external storage devices, magnetic tape and magnetic disk. In fact, when using a mainframe computer it is unlikely that data is written directly to an output device when the computer, for example, is told to print some information. The information will be written to a storage device and then printed at a time that is convenient to the computer. The printer might be busy just at the time when the print instruction is given. The information will, therefore, be stored until the printer is not busy. Computer people call this *spooling*.

We will be looking at the way in which data is written onto magnetic devices in the next chapter when we look at computer files.

*Now work on Assignments 15 and 16 in the* Teacher's Manual, *and on Program C (printer required) on the disk.*

## CHAPTER 5

# Computer Files

## STORAGE AND MEMORY

One of the most useful things that a computer can do is store very large amounts of data in very small spaces. In this chapter we will look at the way computers store data and the hardware that they use for data storage.

When talking about the storage hardware of the computer we need to be clear as to what we mean. In the next chapter we will see that the processing unit of the computer also has storage, or memory, but in this chapter we will be looking at the data that is stored outside the processing unit. This we call *external storage*, whereas the storage that is available in the processing unit we call *internal storage*, or memory.

## INTERNAL MEMORY

The internal memory of a computer is only big enough to hold a limited amount of data, but most computer systems, especially business computer systems, need to store large amounts of data. Internal memory data may also be lost when the machine is turned off.

## EXTERNAL MEMORY

The external storage of a computer is very important. The people who design computer systems have to give a great deal of thought to the way that data is stored for their systems. Some systems need to be able to recall data from external storage very quickly. For example, people wanting to book an airline flight at an airport expect the computer to tell them if a seat is available instantly. In other systems data may not need to be looked up so quickly, and therefore the data can be stored quite differently.

## COMPUTER FILES

Data is kept in a computer's external storage in *files*, just as data on documents is kept in cardboard files in a filing cabinet. The data on computer files, however, cannot be seen in the same way as document files. The data is written onto magnetic tape or magnetic disk and is invisible to the eye. This causes non-computer people a lot of concern, but data written onto magnetic tape or disk is very like data written onto paper. If the data written onto disk or tape was printed out you would be able to see it just as if the data was kept in paper files. It is quite safe, although, as we shall see, it is important that we take steps to make sure we have copies of the files. We should keep copies of data stored on paper as well as on tape or disk.

## RECORDS

What is meant by a file? A file is a place where we keep *records* of things. For example, a business must have a record of each person who works for them. It must keep a record of each of its customers, and of how much money each customer owes. Businesses keep lots of files; stock files, personnel files, customer files, supplier files, and many others. You can see how useful a computer is to a business.

*Now work on Assignment 17 in the* Teacher's Manual.

Each record in a file is full of what some computer people call *data items*, while others call them *fields*, which is rather a strange word for a piece of data. Data items tell us more about the subject of the record. For instance, we might keep a file about our friends, with a record in it for each friend, each record containing data items that describe that person for us. We would have data items such as name, address, sex, colour of hair, height, and, perhaps, indicators to say other things about the friend that we might like to know. It might be useful to know if they are rich, or generous, or rich and generous!

In a payroll file for a business there will be a record for each worker. Each record will contain data items such as the worker's name, address, sex, rate of pay, tax code, and all the other items that are needed to keep track of a worker and to calculate his/her pay each week or month. The records in a customer file will contain data items such as name and address, and will also contain items such as delivery instructions, details of amounts owed, and payments made by the customer.

Businesses need a variety of files in their computer systems.

## MASTER FILES

Files that contain this vital data are called *master files*. Master files must be looked after very carefully, because if the data was lost it would cause a great deal of trouble. It may even cause a business to have to stop processing data, which could cause it to lose a lot of money. For example, it may not be able to send its customers any bills, so it will not receive any money, or it may not be able to pay its workers. You can imagine what effect that would have!

## TRANSACTION FILES

*Transaction files* contain data that is not quite so important. It is usually data that will be added to the data contained in the master files. Computer people call the process of adding transaction data to a master file *updating*. When that has happened the data on the transaction file does not need to be kept any more. If the data on a transaction file is lost there is usually an easy way to find it again.

*Now work on Assignment 18 in the* Teacher's Manual.

An example of transaction data is the information on a cheque paid from a bank account, such as date, account number, amount. At the end of the day the cheque will be posted to the customer's account on the customer's master file so that the bank knows what the new balance for that customer is. If by any chance the transaction file containing the details of the cheque was lost before the customer's file was updated, the bank would still have the cheque, and could use that to put a new transaction on file to replace the one that was lost.

## DUMP FILES

As mentioned earlier, computer systems need copies of master files as a safeguard against the valuable data on those files being lost. The files that are used to copy master files to are called *dump files*.

## SYSTEMS FILES

Computer systems also need files to store all the software that is needed to run the system, to store all the programs that have been written to process the data. These files are called *systems files*. We will look at systems and dump files again in the chapter on operating systems, Chapter 10.

Now we know something about files we can look at the way we store them on magnetic tape or disk.

## FINDING RECORDS ON FILES

When we write files onto a tape or disk we have to do so in such a way that we can get at any of the records we need from the file afterwards. A computer file is like any other file. We would not dream of putting, say, letters in a cardboard file in any old order. How would we find any particular letter we wanted at a later date? Usually we file letters in date order to make them easy to find. Computer people would call the date, therefore, the *key* to a letter.

## RECORD KEYS

Records on computer files need *keys*. You perhaps can see why they are called keys. They enable the computer to find a particular record from a file. They unlock the record, if you like. Each record in a file, therefore, needs a data item, or data items, that provide that key. They are often called *key fields*. When the computer is looking for a record in a file it will look for the key field to find the record.

A file of your friends might use their names as the key field. A personnel file will probably use some sort of works number as the key field. A customer file will probably use an account number.

## SERIAL FILES

The easiest way to write records onto a computer file is one after another. This is known as *serial* storage. When reading records from the file, or *accessing* them, as computer people say, the computer simply reads one record after another looking at the key fields until it reaches the record it needs. This causes problems, unless the records are in some sort of order. If they are not, every time the computer wants to find a record it has to go back to the beginning of the file and read every record again until it reaches the one it needs. If it was a tape file it would have to wait for the tape to be rewound to the beginning. This is obviously not sensible. Serial files are always sorted to some sort of order, usually ascending order of the key field or fields. They are then called *sequential* files. The transaction files that are used to update sequential master files are sorted to the same order. If they were not, the computer would have to go back to the start of the master file each time it wanted to find a record to update it.

Although serial files can be written onto magnetic tape or disk, magnetic tape can only hold serial-type files. This is because of the way that a tape device, or *drive* as it is called, works. The tape passes under a read/write head, and once a piece of tape has passed under the head it cannot be read from or written to again. Therefore it is only possible to write or read one record after another onto or from the tape.

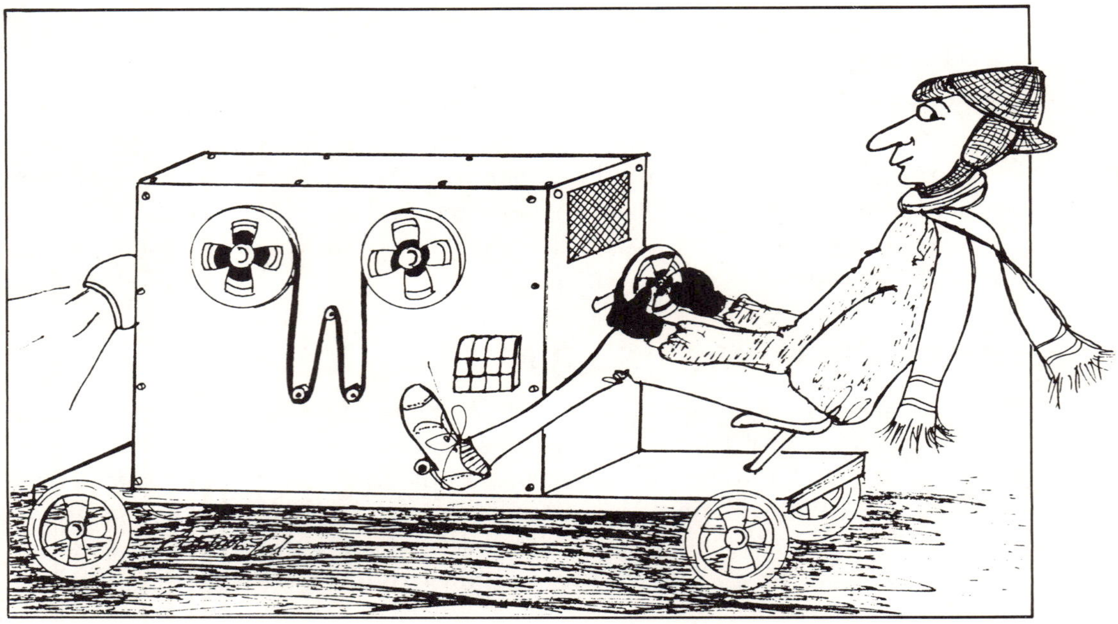

Tape drive being used

## UPDATING SERIAL FILES

In order to update a tape file the old tape is read, updated, and the new version written onto another tape drive. This fact does have a good point. It means that there is always a copy of a master tape file, because every time it is updated the old copy of the file still remains. The updating of sequential master files is known as *father/son updating*, for what should be obvious reasons.

It is sensible to keep large sequential files on magnetic tape. Magnetic tape and cassettes for computers are just like tape recorder tapes or cassettes. They are cheaper than disks and hold large amounts of data. Reels of tape for mainframe computers and minicomputers are much cheaper than the disk packs we will look at shortly, and take up less storage space.

## DISK FILES

Magnetic disks are known as *direct access devices*. They are different from magnetic tapes, but you can see that just by looking at them. They look like gramophone records, and come in a range of different sizes.

## FLOPPY DISKS

Microcomputers typically use small, 'floppy' disks, floppy because they bend very easily. They are made of thin plastic. Those generally used are like single playing gramophone records. They can hold up to 500 000 characters or bytes of data. It is important to note that the read/write head of a floppy disk drive touches the floppy disk. As a result, the disk must eventually wear out.

## HARD DISKS

Larger computers tend to use hard disks, although they are also available for microcomputers. These look more like long playing gramophone records. Although some computers use single hard disks, they usually come in *packs* (see Fig. 5.1). Several disks are linked by a central spindle so that there are two, six, eleven, or more disks one on top of the other.

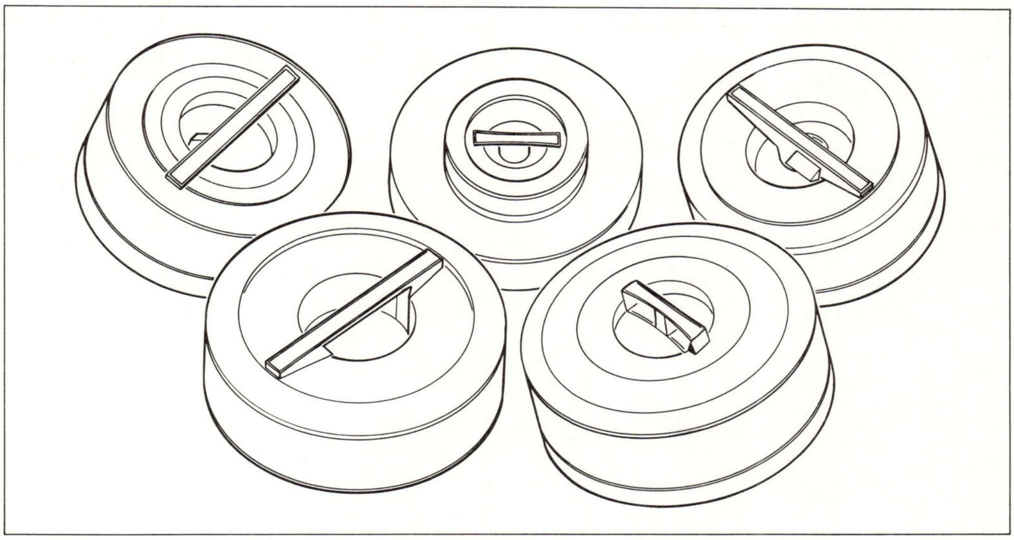

**Figure 5.1** *Disk packs*

The disk packs are held in *disk drives*. Some disk drives have the disk packs fixed in them so that the storage on them is always *on-line*, or available, to the computer. Some disk drives use *exchangeable* disk packs, which means that the disk packs can be removed and replaced by others with different files on them. Hard disks and disk packs can hold millions of characters or bytes of data, large disk packs hundreds of millions.

Unlike the floppy disk drive, the read/write head of a hard disk drive does not touch the disk itself. As a result, the hard disk has a long lifetime.

## READ/WRITE HEADS

When a disk or disk pack is loaded into a disk drive and the drive is turned on, the disks revolve and read/write heads are moved over the disks. This is what makes magnetic disk storage so different from magnetic tape. Because the disks revolve and the read/write heads move over the disks, we do not need to write records onto the disks one after another or to read them from the disks one after another. Serial files *can* be written onto disks, but it is also possible to store files in different ways.

## TRACKS

The surface of a disk is covered in a series of *tracks*. The outside track is large, and each track from the outside to the inside is smaller than the previous one. We call them *concentric*.

## CYLINDERS

On a disk pack with more than one disk there are several read/write heads on an *arm*, one for each disk surface. The outside surfaces are not used. They are just dust covers. Each time the read/write head moves, the computer can read from the same track on each of the disk surfaces. The track that can be read by the computer each time the read/write head moves is known as a *cylinder*. To help you understand, imagine writing records serially onto a disk pack. The computer starts writing records on the first track in the cylinder, which is the outside track on the top disk. When that track is full of records the computer will then start writing on the outside track of the next disk down, using the second read/write head. When that is full it will write on the next disk down, and so on, until the outside track on the bottom disk is full. The first cylinder is then full, and the read/write head will move on to the next cylinder ready to continue writing from its top track (see Fig. 5.2).

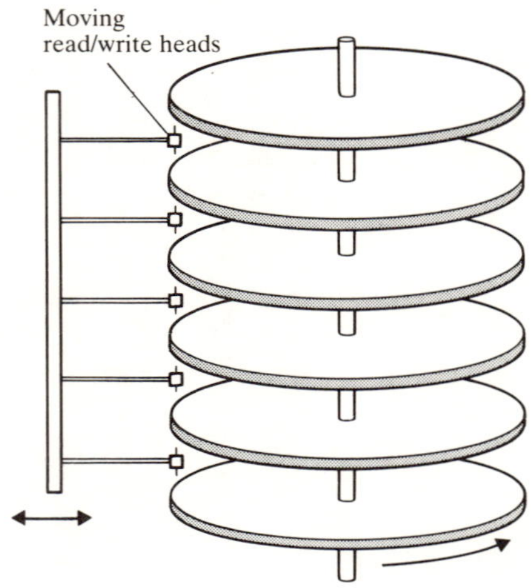


**Figure 5.2** *Moving read/write heads*

So you can see that a single disk is divided up into tracks, and a disk pack is divided into cylinders. To complicate matters further some systems subdivide the disks into smaller chunks or *sectors*, although the reason for this is not important here. The disks revolve, and the read/write heads can move backwards and forwards across the disks. Very different from magnetic tape isn't it?

## FINDING RECORDS ON DISK FILES

The important thing about disks is that the computer can move the read/write heads to particular tracks on any disk. It is not necessary to read one record after another. If we know the track a record is on, we can go straight to the record. This is what we mean by *direct access*. It is possible to go straight to a record on a disk or disk pack by finding out where it is on the disks.

## RANDOM ACCESS

There are two ways of locating a record. The first way is to make the key field of a record point to where it is on the disk or disk pack. The key field can be arranged so that it tells the computer the track where the record will be stored, or the *address* of the record. Usually it is not convenient for key fields to be disk addresses, so the computer has to do some arithmetic on the key field to change it into a disk address. Computer people call this *hashing*. They also call this way of getting at records on a disk pack *random access*, which seems strange, because there is nothing random about it.

## USING AN INDEX

The other way of finding a record on a disk, and probably the way used most, is by using an *index*. This is just like an index in a book. The computer writes another file on the disk, and all that file shows is the key fields of the records in the file in order, as in a sequential file. Against each key field is the address of the record for that key on the disks. When the computer wants to find a record it looks through the key fields in the index until it finds the one it wants. It then has, next to the key field, the address of the record and can go straight to it.

Using an index

Not only can the computer find records very quickly using the index, it can also find records sequentially. This is because the key fields are in order in the index. The computer can read through the index *sequentially*. Indexed files are often called *index sequential* files.

## WHY USE DIRECT ACCESS FILES?

Direct access files are needed for many computer systems. Think about an airline booking system again. A person wanting details about a flight at an airport cannot wait for the computer to read all the way through a sequential file on magnetic tape. The computer must be able to go straight to the records for any flight. You can probably think of many other computer systems where direct access of records is necessary, a bank's cashpoint system, for example.

## UPDATING IN PLACE

There is one problem with direct access files on disks that you should remember. When a magnetic tape file is updated the old copy of the file still remains, which gives some security. Direct access files are updated *in place*, which means that the computer reads in a record, changes it as it is updated, and then writes it back onto the disk in the same place that it read it from. The old record is therefore lost. This means that it is very important that direct access files are copied often. It is best to make a copy of the file every time it is updated.

## OTHER STORAGE DEVICES

You will probably see other external storage devices around. Some microcomputers now use very small microdisks, for example, and it will be interesting to see what sort of storage devices we may see in the future. In this chapter, we have looked at the main types of external storage device and file that you are likely to come across.

## WORD PROCESSING

It is appropriate in a chapter on computer files to talk about *word processing*. This is because word processing is dependent on the computer filing large quantities of information in a small space and calling up that information very quickly.

The word processor has changed the way that letters, reports, and other office documents are produced and filed. Using a word processor is not like using a typewriter. The person typing sees the document being typed on the VDU screen. Mistakes can be quickly and easily corrected by back spacing and replacing the previous text. Words, sentences, or whole sections of text can be removed and replaced. The text can be rearranged if the order in which it was typed is not liked. Extra text can be added. The text can be stored on disk to be returned to later. The document does not need to be printed on paper until the typist is sure that it is correct.

In offices, standard letters can be typed and stored away on disk to be called up for printing any time they are needed. In addition, names and addresses of people with whom the business deals can be kept on separate files. Their names and addresses can be automatically put onto the letters as they are printed by the word processor.

This book was typed on a word processor. You can imagine how that has helped me. I have been able to read through the text and alter bits that I did not like at any time. The whole book is now held on four small floppy disks (see Fig. 5.3), and it can still be easily revised as required.

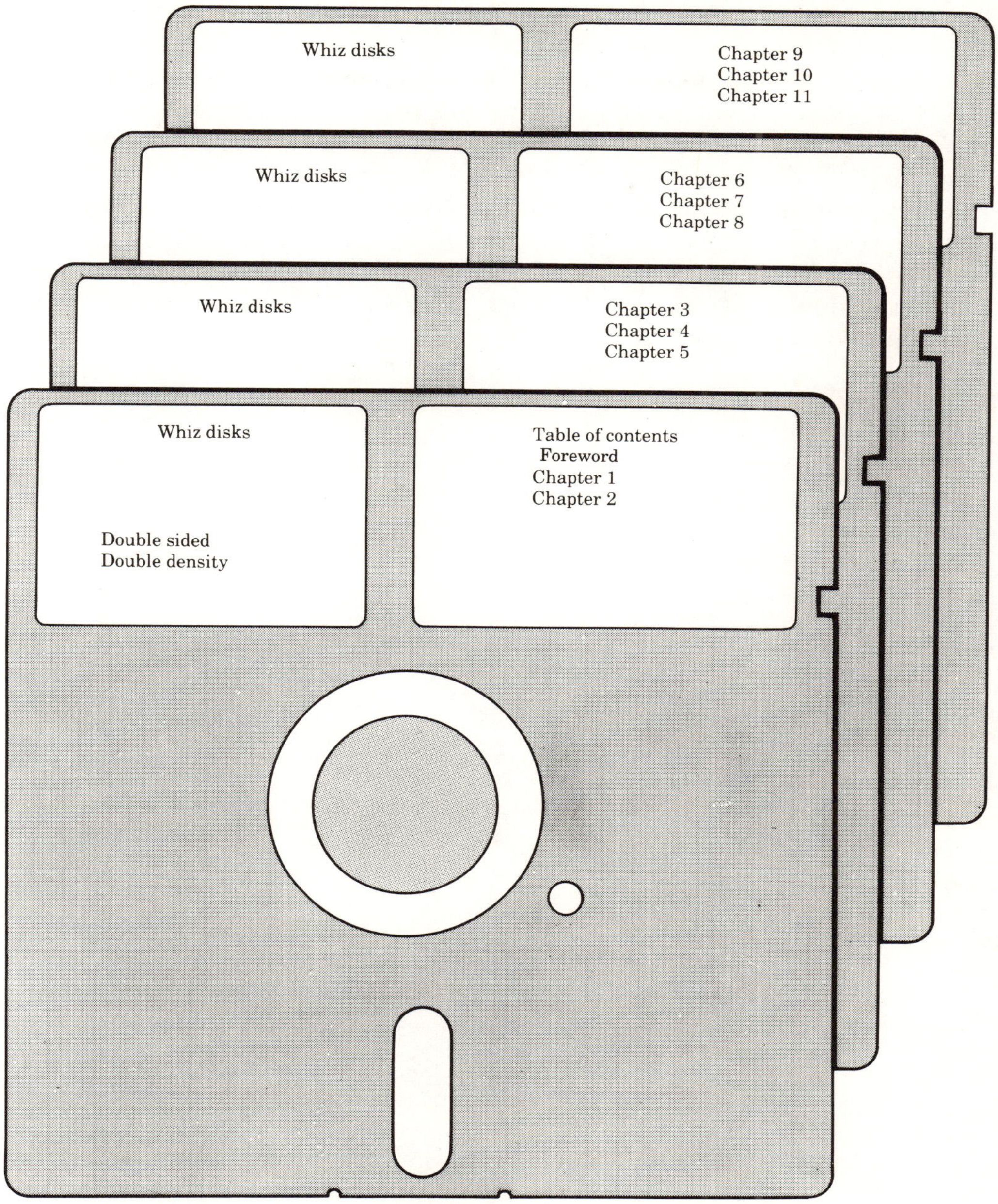


**Figure 5.3** *Book held on four floppy disks*

*Now work on Assignment 19 in the* Teacher's Manual.

## DATABASES

Finally, we cannot leave a chapter on computer files without mentioning *databases*. Many businesses file their data in databases these days. A database is really a central file in which the data for all the computer systems within the business is kept. This means that all data is available to everybody who wants to look at it.

Without a database, separate files have to be kept for each system. It is difficult for the data from each system to be made available to people who do not use the system. It means that managers cannot easily get information from all systems when they need to, and obviously they do need to if they are to manage the business well.

Databases file all data in one place. They are managed by special software that looks after the data items and allows access to them as and when required. The data items are not filed in records in the way we saw earlier in this chapter. They are often filed in lists, so that similar data items are kept together in the database. The data items are linked in various ways so that they can be organized into records when that is needed. However, because similar data items are kept together it is easy for managers to get selected information from the database. The database management software usually provides special enquiry systems for managers.

*Now work on Assignment 20 in the* Teacher's Manual, *and on Program G on the disk.*

## CHAPTER 6

# The Processing Unit

## PRINCIPLE PARTS OF A COMPUTER

The computer has various component parts, among the most important of which are the *processor* and the *memory*. The processor contains the *arithmetic and logic unit* (ALU) where it performs calculations and makes decisions. It also contains the *control unit* which supervises all the electronic operations of the computer. The memory, sometimes called *internal storage* or the *random access memory* (RAM), is used by the computer to store data. The data may be information input by the user, the results of calculations, or the program itself.

## CHIPS

The memory of a computer consists mostly of microelectronic integrated circuits called *memory chips*. Each chip is a complex and microscopically small electronic circuit, produced by a complicated photochemical process on a 'chip' of pure silicon. Each circuit contains a large number of electronic 'switches' (usually several thousand). Any switch can be 'on' (represented by a high voltage) or 'off' (represented by a low voltage). Thus each of these switches can stand for a digit; a '1' (on) or a '0' (off), which in turn is the electronic equivalent of a *binary number*. The binary system of arithmetic (base two) uses only the two digits '0' and '1'.

## BITS AND BYTES

Because they can easily be represented electronically, binary numbers are used inside the computer to store all data. Each binary digit is called a *bit* (short for Binary digIT), and eight bits are known as a *byte* (a contraction of 'by eight'). One byte is the smallest unit of information handled by the computer, and can be used to represent any number up to 255. Larger numbers are handled by using several bytes to represent them. The processor uses binary numbers of fixed length, either 8, 16, or 32 bits long depending on the type and power of the computer.

*Now work on Assignment 21 in the* Teacher's Manual.

## RAM AND ROM

Many types of chip are used in the microcomputer, but the two most important are *memory chips* and the *microprocessor chip*. Data and programs are stored on the memory chips. Some of the memory is called ROM, which is short for *read only memory*, and some is called RAM, which is short for *random access memory*.

### *ROM*

ROM is a permanent store of information. As its name implies, you can only read data from this memory. It cannot be overwritten by other data. ROM is typically used to hold such programs as the computer's operating system (see Chapter 10). It also often contains a program called an interpreter which translates programs that are typed into the computer (see Chapter 9).

### *RAM*

RAM is temporary storage. Information can be read from or overwritten by other information. Programs that we write are loaded into RAM. The data that is read into those programs from peripheral devices is held in RAM while it is processed.

The memory chips are covered in memory locations where a byte of information is stored. The memory locations are numbered so that the microprocessor can find the information stored there. The number of each memory location is called its *address*. The addresses of memory locations start at zero and move up numerically, so that every location has its own individual address.

## BUSES

When the computer is working the locations in the memory chips contain program instructions and data. Instructions and data, however, are acted upon in the microprocessor chip, so there has to be some way of moving instructions and data between the memory chips and the processor. Information is transferred between memory and the processor on *buses*. Buses are sets of wires. I say wires, but they are really tracks printed on a printed circuit board. You can think of them as wires.

There are three buses between the memory chips and the processor: the *address* bus, the *data* bus, and the *control* bus.

The address bus shows where information is in the memory. It usually has at least 16 parallel wires, but is much bigger on most modern computers.

The data bus transfers bytes of data and instructions between the memory and the processor. It has at least eight parallel wires because information is stored in memory in at least eight bit bytes. We will see how information is stored in bytes later in the chapter.

The control bus transfers signals between the processor and memory, signals such as whether information is to be read from or written to memory.

## THE MICROPROCESSOR CHIP

The microprocessor chip is covered with control circuits which organize the way the computer works. It has an ALU where all calculations are carried out and where all decisions are made. The circuitry within the ALU contains *logic gates* which are used to carry out the instructions received from the programs. These gates open and close to let electronic signals through according to the binary inputs they receive, in the form of instructions.

## REGISTERS

The microprocessor has *registers*, which are like memory chips. They are used to store data and instructions while they are being worked on. They also hold the addresses of data which are needed from the memory. Some of the registers do special jobs, and so have special names.

### *Program counter*

One register is called the *program counter*. It holds the binary address of the next byte of data or the next instruction to be fetched from memory if the program is to work in the correct sequence. When a program starts to run, the program counter is set to the address of the first instruction in the program. This is put onto the address bus so that the instruction can be fetched from the memory chips. While it is being fetched the program counter is increased by one so that it contains the address of the next byte of the program. This cycle continues until the program ends, except where a jump instruction (see Chapter 9) changes the contents of the program counter completely.

### *Instruction register*

Each time an instruction is fetched into the processor from memory, the operation code is put into an eight bit register called the *instruction register*. It remains there until the control circuits have carried out the instruction, when it is replaced by the operation code of the next instruction.

### *Accumulator*

The *accumulator* is a register used by the ALU. It is called the accumulator because it holds the results of additions that take place in the ALU before the results are put into memory. In some arithmetic, such as multiplication, the calculation is a series of separate additions, so the result in the accumulator grows and grows. In other words, it accumulates.

### *Status register*

The *status* or *flag* register is again an eight bit register. Each bit is used as an indicator by the ALU to show that particular things have happened. Each bit can be thought of as a flag that is raised or lowered, or turned on or off, as the events occur. For example, one of the flags is called the 'carry' flag. If an addition takes place in the ALU, and the result of it is too big to fit into the accumulator, this flag is raised.

The other registers in the microprocessor are working registers used for temporary storage of data. There are not many of them, and they are the only places in the processor where data can be stored, so there is a lot of traffic on the buses between memory and the processor.

## OPERATION CODES

The first byte of any instruction represents the operation code (or *opcode*) of that instruction. The operation code governs the action taken by the central processor when executing a particular instruction. The operation codes recognized by one type of processor represent that processor's *instruction set.*

## INTERFACES

Data not only flows between memory and the processor, however. Data also has to flow between the processing unit and input, output, and storage devices. There is a problem here, because not all of these peripheral devices send and receive data as binary signals. For example, data received from a keyboard on a VDU is binary because a key is either pressed or it isn't pressed. However, data received from a heat sensor is always there, the temperature just goes up or down. This type of signal is called an *analogue* signal.

### *Interface chips*

To get round this problem special chips are used. These are called *interface* chips. They convert the electrical signals from peripheral devices to binary codes as data is input, and back again as data is output. Interface chips cope with data being sent to and from the processing unit in other than binary codes.

There is another problem when passing data between the processing unit and peripherals. Some output devices do not work as fast as the processor. A printer is a good example. A processor sends data to a printer at a speed of thousands of bytes a second, much faster than the printer can put the characters on paper. One way to overcome this problem is to use areas of RAM to store the characters while they are waiting to be printed. These storage areas are called *buffers.*

Having looked at the memory chips and the microprocessor chip we will now see how information can be stored in memory.

## BINARY NUMBERS

We have already seen that the computer uses bits, or binary digits, as its basic storage unit. It will be useful, therefore, to know a little more about the binary numbering system.

The binary system only uses two numbers, zero and one. In the decimal numbering system that we are used to you 'carry' to the next position when 10 is reached, that is $9 + 1 = 10$ (one '10' and no units). In the binary system you 'carry' when you reach two, that is $1 + 1 = 10$ (one 'two' and no units). You count like this: 0, 1, 10, 11, 100, 101, 111, and so on. In other words, $1 + 1 = 10$, $11 + 1 = 100$, and $10 =$ decimal number 2, while $100 =$ decimal number 4.

In a byte of memory consisting of eight bytes, the binary number 11111111 can be stored. This is number 255 in the decimal system. Think of each bit as being a binary number like this:

bit 0 = 1
bit 1 = 2
bit 2 = 4
bit 3 = 8
bit 4 = 16
bit 5 = 32
bit 6 = 64
bit 7 = 128
Add them all up = 255

Most computer people probably think of the bits in a byte the other way up, with bit number one being at the bottom and bit number eight being at the top. You can see that the value of each bit doubles.

*Now work on Assignment 22 in the* Teacher's Manual.

## HEXADECIMAL NUMBERS

You can also see that in the first four bits of the byte the decimal number 15 can be stored, that is 1 + 2 + 4 + 8. You can think of these bits as being the one bit, the two bit, the four bit, and the eight bit. Another numbering system that is used by computers is the *hexadecimal* system. In this system you 'carry' when the number 16 is reached, that is 10 (one '16' and no units) = decimal number 16. The numbers in the hexadecimal system are:

0 1 2 3 4 5 6 7 8 9 A B C D E F.

*Note*: letters are used for numbers greater than 9 (A = 10, B = 11, etc.). The reason is fairly obvious. If we used 10 (ten) rather than A this would lead to confusion as we have already seen that 10 in the hexadecimal system is 16 in decimal. In hexadecimal:

F + 1 = 10, and
1F + 1 = 20.

Hexadecimal number 20 = decimal number 32.

By using the hexadecimal system, two numbers can be held in one byte of storage. Some computers do hold data like this. Numbers stored in this way are called *packed* decimal numbers because two have been packed into one byte.

## STORING CHARACTERS

The point about storing numbers in binary or hexadecimal is that a much larger number can be stored in a byte of memory than when numbers are stored as decimal numbers. The highest decimal number that can be stored in a byte of memory is the number nine. This is because the computer

| | Binary | | | | Binary | | |
|---|---|---|---|---|---|---|---|
| Character | Zone | Digit | Hexadecimal | Character | Zone | Digit | Hexadecimal |
| 0 | 0101 | 0000 | 50 | J | 1010 | 1010 | AA |
| 1 | 0101 | 0001 | 51 | K | 1010 | 1011 | AB |
| 2 | 0101 | 0010 | 52 | L | 1010 | 1100 | AC |
| 3 | 0101 | 0011 | 53 | M | 1010 | 1101 | AD |
| 4 | 0101 | 0100 | 54 | N | 1010 | 1110 | AE |
| 5 | 0101 | 0101 | 55 | O | 1010 | 1111 | AF |
| 6 | 0101 | 0110 | 56 | P | 1011 | 0000 | B0 |
| 7 | 0101 | 0111 | 57 | Q | 1011 | 0001 | B1 |
| 8 | 0101 | 1000 | 58 | R | 1011 | 0010 | B2 |
| 9 | 0101 | 1001 | 59 | S | 1011 | 0011 | B3 |
| A | 1010 | 0001 | A1 | T | 1011 | 0100 | B4 |
| B | 1010 | 0010 | A2 | U | 1011 | 0101 | B5 |
| C | 1010 | 0011 | A3 | V | 1011 | 0110 | B6 |
| D | 1010 | 0100 | A4 | W | 1011 | 0111 | B7 |
| E | 1010 | 0101 | A5 | X | 1011 | 1000 | B8 |
| F | 1010 | 0110 | A6 | Y | 1011 | 1001 | B9 |
| G | 1010 | 0111 | A7 | Z | 1011 | 1010 | BA |
| H | 1010 | 1000 | A8 | | | | |
| I | 1010 | 1001 | A9 | | | | |

**Figure 6.1** *Numeric and alphabetic characters in ASCII–8*

stores decimal numbers in the same way as it stores other characters such as letters or special characters like a comma, asterisk (*), or ampersand (&). A computer stores characters in its memory by using the bits within each byte as codes. A combination of bits turned on within a byte represents a character.

A coding system used by many computers is the ASCII code of the American Standards Institute (American Standard Code for Information Interchange). This is pronounced 'ass-key'. This system uses the full eight bits of a byte to represent a character. Figure 6.1 shows the bit patterns and codes for each capital letter and the decimal numbers 0 to 9. Other bit combinations in these codes are used to represent other characters, like the special characters I mentioned before and non-capital letters.

The microelectronics of the computer are outside of the scope of this book, but hopefully this chapter has given you a small insight into the workings of the processing unit.

*Now work on Assignment 23 in the* Teacher's Manual, *and Programs D, F and K on the disk.*

## CHAPTER 7

# Computer Systems

## WHAT IS A COMPUTER SYSTEM?

We have seen what a computer is. Now let us see what we mean by a computer system.

*Now work on Assignment 24 in the* Teacher's Manual.

A computer system is a mixture of hardware and software. This is a simple way of looking at it, and it will need more explanation. Normally people get a computer and use it for many of their requirements. For instance, a business might get a fairly large mainframe computer and use it to produce bills for its customers, calculate the pay for its workers, keep records of its stocks of materials and goods, and so on. Each of the jobs that that computer does would be called a *system.* The computer people within the business would refer to them as 'the billing system', 'the payroll system', and 'the stock system'.

## HOME SYSTEMS

If you buy yourself a home computer and decide to write some programs to, say, manage your mum's deep freeze or keep your dad's bank account straight, you will then have your own computer systems. You will probably call them 'the freezer system' or 'the bank system'.

## BUSINESS SYSTEMS

When businesses first used computers and found them ideal for many of the tedious jobs businesses have to do, computers were very expensive and very big. Most businesses could only afford one computer and ran all their systems on the one machine. Over the years things changed. Computers became very much cheaper and smaller. Businesses started to realize how powerful computers were. They found that they could do jobs with computers that were impossible to do without them. They also found that there were different types of computer, and that some were suitable for some types of system, and some for others. Businesses can now buy different computers for different systems, not running all their systems on the same computer. Computer people call a computer that is used for a particular system a *dedicated machine.*

You will now find that larger businesses will usually have more than one computer. Some will have many. The different computers will do different jobs within the business, or they will be dedicated to different systems.

## LARGE SYSTEMS

A large chain of stores is likely to have an enormous computer system, with several mainframe computers. There may be hundreds of bar-code readers in their shops connected to the computers, with miles of telephone links between the shops and the computers. This hardware will be used to control customers' checkouts and stocks in shops. These computers will spend all their time looking after the checkouts and stock system, so all the other systems that the chain of stores has will need other computers of varying sizes, mainframe, mini, and micro.

You can probably think of other systems that need dedicated hardware. Think about an airline booking system, for example.

In many businesses, though, the variety of computers now available and their decreasing price, has meant that computers can be obtained for particular systems instead of all the systems being run on the same computer. I know of one business where a new computer is bought for each system that is introduced.

Today it is possible for a business to look at a system and easily get a machine to suit that system. Therefore, the people who design computer systems within businesses often decide upon the computer hardware to buy for a system, as well as making a decision as to what software needs to be written for the system.

*Now work on Assignment 25 in the* Teacher's Manual.

## SYSTEMS ANALYSTS

The people who design computer systems are called *systems analysts*. The reason for this is because they look at systems within a business to find out just what the systems should be doing. In other words they analyse the systems. They also design new computer systems to replace the old ones, but nevertheless they tend to be called systems analysts rather than systems designers.

The systems analysts do a very important job. We can break down what they do into several stages.

### *Feasibility studies*

Usually the first thing a systems analyst will do when asked to look at a system is what is known as a *feasibility study*. This is a first look at the old system to see if it is worth changing. The change may mean taking a system that does not use a computer, getting a computer for the system, and writing all the software to make the system work. It may mean changing an old computer system to work on a new, perhaps more up-to-date, computer. It may just mean rewriting some of the computer programs to make the system work in a slightly different way.

The systems analyst looks to see if the changes are worth while. What costs could be saved by making the changes, or the extra money that the business could make by being more efficient because of the changes. It may be possible that the business could improve its image by using a new, more up-to-date computer system.

*Now work on Assignment 26 in the* Teacher's Manual.

## *Fact finding*

Once it has been decided that the changes are worth while the systems analyst then looks at the old system to see how it works and, more importantly, to see what information the users of the system need to do their jobs properly. It is necessary to look at the data they use, the files they keep, the forms they fill in and the reports they have to produce, and to go round the user's department asking questions, and so on. The systems analyst will also collect up forms and reports so that he or she can see exactly what is going on and what is needed from the system. This stage of the systems analyst's job is usually called the *fact-finding* stage.

Systems analyst investigating

## *Systems design*

After the fact-finding stage the systems analyst is ready to *design* the new system. A decision will have to be made on the way the data will be input to the system, the files that the system will need, and the information that the system must produce. This will involve the design of forms and reports, the selection of input devices (see Chapter 3), and decisions on how data will be held on and retrieved from storage devices (see Chapter 5).

The computer programmers will have to be told what software needs to be written to make the systems work. This information is written by the systems analyst in *program specifications*, which are then given to the programmers so that they can write their programs.

*Now work on Assignment 27 in the* Teacher's Manual.

### *Systems implementation*

The final stage in getting the new system ready is known as the *implementation* stage. While the computer programs are being written, the systems analyst will be doing other jobs that must be carried out before the system will work. The staff who will use the system must be trained in their new jobs. These new jobs may be strange to them, like using VDUs or filling in special types of form. The forms that the system will use must be ordered. Moreover, it will be sensible to keep an eye on the programmers to see that the programs are tested well to ensure that they work when the system goes into use. The systems analyst may write some data to test the system, or use some real data that has already gone through the old system.

One of the most important jobs will be to create the master files for the new system. Master files are explained in Chapter 5. If the old system is not already running on a computer the data that must be on the master files for the new system will have to be put into the computer system. There may be many hundreds of records to go onto the master files for the new system, so this could be a long and difficult job, involving many people and much checking of data. The new system cannot run until this job has been done.

### *Parallel running*

When all these stages have been completed the new system is ready to be used. If it is possible, though, the old system will not be abandoned at this stage. Often the old and new systems will run side by side for a period of time until the systems analyst is sure that the new system works properly. This is called *parallel running*.

### *Direct changeover*

Sometimes the new system is so different from the old system that parallel running is not possible. For example, the first computer airline booking system was so different from the manual system it replaced that it was impossible to run the old and new side by side to compare the results. In cases like these the new system must begin running straight away, taking over the old system without parallel running. This is called *direct changeover*. Thorough testing of such systems is very important.

So, you can now see what we mean when we talk about computer systems. Some computer systems are vast and complex, made up of large amounts of special hardware and perhaps many computers. At the same time some computer systems are small, with several of them working on the same computer. We will look again at some examples of large computer systems in Chapter 10 when we look at computer networks.

*Now work on Assignment 28 in the* Teacher's Manual, *and on Program B on the disk.*

## CHAPTER 8

# Data Processing

## WHAT THE COMPUTER IS USED FOR

Now that we have seen what the computer is, we will consider what it is used for, apart from playing games. The computer is used for *data processing*, a term that has now become closely linked with the computer. Businesses, however, were processing data long before the computer came along to make it easier. As soon as a business starts producing goods or services it has to start processing data.

Data processing means turning *raw data* into *information*. A business making goods to sell will be turning raw materials into those goods by putting them through a manufacturing process. It cannot carry on that manufacturing process, however, without processing data.

## BUSINESS DATA PROCESSING

As soon as a business receives orders for goods, it has raw data to process. From those orders the business will want information so that it knows what goods to make and when they are required. It can then plan its production and buying of materials.

As a business grows, the amount of data it receives, or needs to store, grows. Its information requirements also become more complex. It will need to know much more about the sales of its products and the market it is selling to so that it can plan its greatly increased production and marketing operations.

Businesses do not exist in a vacuum. They are part of an economy, and over the years the economy has become more complex. These days a business needs to provide much information about its activities to other organizations, particularly government departments.

Business data processing operations have now become very important. In fact, in many businesses, the processing of data to produce information has probably become as important as the processing of raw materials to produce goods.

The computer has made data processing much easier. Its speed and storage capabilities have helped businesses produce the information they require quickly and effectively. Computers have enabled people to have available information that could not have been produced using manual data processing systems. When we talk about computer systems, we are really talking about these systems of processing data to give people and businesses the information they require to be able to operate properly. Let us look at some examples of data processing systems.

## HOME DATA PROCESSING

It is not only a business that can benefit from the data processing capabilities of the computer. A family can also have data to process. For example, many homes now have a freezer to store the family food. You could write a

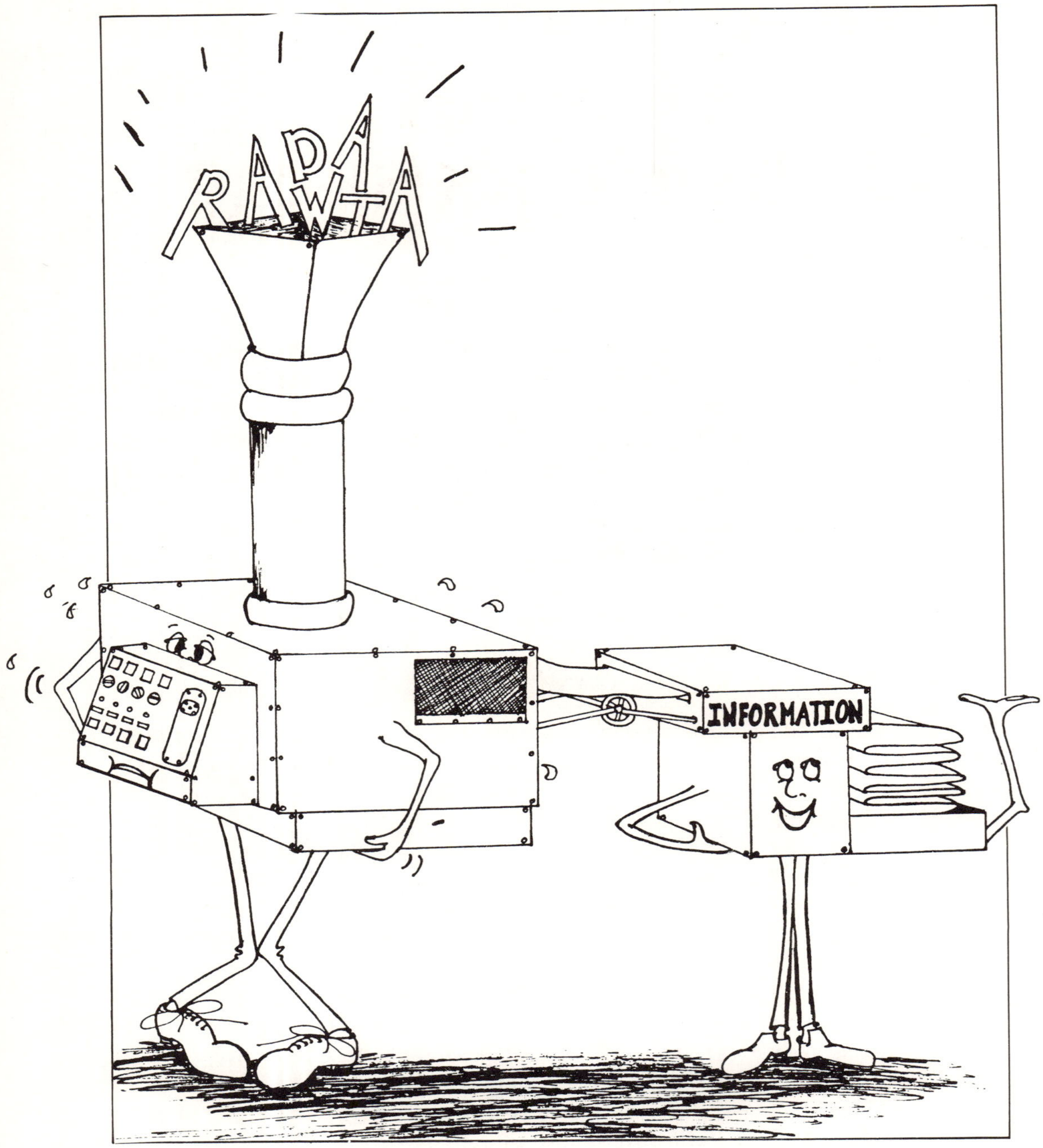


Information from raw data

data processing system, to manage this food storage, for a home computer. The data to be input to the system is:

1. Details of items put into the freezer, with the dates they were stored and the length of time they can be kept for.
2. Details of items removed from the freezer.

The details of items held in the freezer could be stored on the computer's storage device. From this data there is a range of useful information available. The system could advise which package of a particular food item should be used first when an item is needed from the freezer for a meal. It could show when items are about to overrun their storage life. It could show when stock of particular items is low and replenishment of those items is required, even producing shopping lists if required. It could even make estimates of how long the food in the freezer would last the family in the event of an emergency.

Business giving information to government

If the prices of items were also entered to the system, the system could show the value of all the food stored in the freezer. This would be useful information if, say, the freezer broke down and it was necessary to make an insurance claim for the contents. I expect that you can think of other useful information that could be produced by a freezer management data processing system. You can perhaps also realize the limitations of the smallest home computer if you want to use it for data processing.

*Now work on Assignment 29 in the* Teacher's Manual.

## A PAYROLL SYSTEM EXAMPLE

What about a business data processing system? All businesses must pay their employees. The raw data input to a payroll system includes the hours worked by the employees. Data about the employees, such as their pay and tax rates and any deductions to be made from their pay, will be held on the computer's storage devices.

From this data the business requires information to show on the employees' payslips how much they have earned. They require information about the tax deducted from employees' pay to forward to the Inland Revenue. They require information about the number of notes and coins to be collected from the bank to make up the employees' pay packets.

In addition to this sort of information, the business can also get information on the cost of labour involved in making its products. It can find out if departments are working within allowable expense budgets, whether excess overtime is being worked in some areas of the business, and other valuable facts to help management.

In a large business, with perhaps thousands of employees, there is a great deal of data to be input and stored. There are many complex and repetitive tasks to be performed on the data, and a large amount of information to be produced. You can see why the computer and its peripheral devices is a useful tool for such a data processing system.

## BATCH PROCESSING

There are basically two different types of data processing system. Some data is processed at regular times. The data going into the system is col-

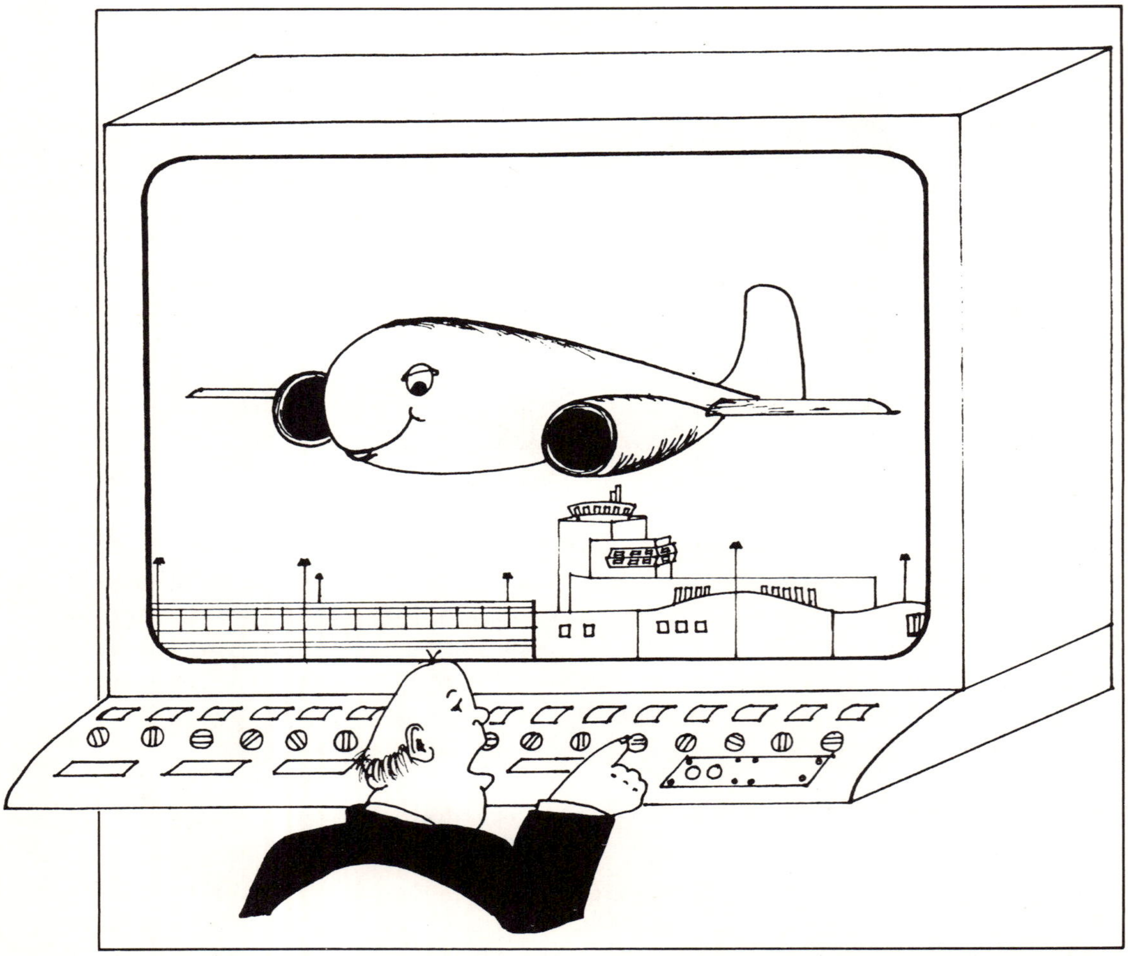

*Airline terminal*

lected over a period of time, or until a certain amount of it has been received, and then that amount of data is input to the computer and processed by it all at the same time. In fact, a *batch* of data is processed at a time. You can perhaps see why this sort of processing is known as *batch processing*. Most businesses, for example, will process the input to the payroll system in a batch. The employees clocking-in cards will be collected up just before pay day, and the hours worked put into the system to produce pay advices and all the other necessary output as one batch. Similarly, the business might process the orders it receives from customers once a day, or perhaps every time it has received 200 orders. Your mother may enter details of items going into the deep freeze after doing the shopping each week. Many data processing systems lend themselves to batch processing methods.

*Now work on Assignment 30 in the* Teacher's Manual.

## REAL-TIME PROCESSING

There are some data processing systems, however, where batch processing is not a suitable method of processing the data. Some systems require that data is processed immediately the transaction that creates the data occurs. For these sorts of system it is essential that up-to-date information is always available.

Suppose an airline has a data processing system to keep records of bookings on their various flights. There may be booking offices in different places all using the system, wanting instant information about flights and available seats for prospective passengers and wanting to make bookings for those seats. When a booking is made from any office, that information must be available to the other offices so that they do not book the same seats. The data from the booking must, therefore, be processed immediately.

Many banks now have cashpoints outside their buildings where customers can queue, often in the rain, for money rather than in the warmth and comfort of the building itself, but it also means they can obtain money when the bank is closed. There are limitations to the amount of money a customer can withdraw and on the number of withdrawals a customer may make in a day. It follows that when a customer does make a withdrawal, the data processing system controlling the cashpoints must immediately record the fact.

*Now work on Assignment 31 in the* Teacher's Manual.

These sorts of data processing system, where data is processed the moment it enters the system, are known as *real-time* systems. The data is processed in 'real time', that is now, immediately.

## A CONTROL SYSTEM

Here is an example of another real-time system which involves the use of a different type of data. Suppose we used a small computer system to control the heating of a house. The computer would detect the temperature through sensors positioned at various places through the house. This data must be processed immediately to turn on radiators when the temperature falls below a certain level to increase the heat output. This is a good example of a real-time system.

The computer is used for all sorts of system. We refer to these systems as applications. We talked about a 'freezer application', a 'payroll application', and an 'airline booking' application earlier in this chapter.

## OTHER DATA PROCESSING APPLICATIONS

Let us take a quick look at some other applications for which computers are used. Businesses use computers for accounting applications. Computers keep records of the amounts that the business owes to its suppliers, and the amounts that its customers owe the business. Records are kept of the money that must be paid to government departments, such as the Inland Revenue and customs and excise. Accounts for the company accountant are printed by the computer.

The computer helps businesses to make their products more efficiently. Stock control applications make sure that the business knows when it needs to buy more goods or materials and help it decide the amount it needs to buy. Production control applications help managers to schedule machines and people on the factory floor so that goods are made efficiently and resources are used in the best possible way.

Computers are used by banks and building societies to keep records of loans and the amounts held in the accounts of their customers.

Insurance companies use computers to hold details of their customers' policies and premiums. They also find that computers are useful tools for calculating what premiums there should be on policies.

Computers are also used for controlling traffic flows in cities, robots in factories, and electricity output from power stations. Some organizations use computers to make decisions for them through what are known as *expert systems*, creating artificial intelligence for the computer.

As was said in the first chapter of this book, you will find computers widely in use these days.

*Now work on Assignment 32 in the* Teacher's Manual, *and on Program E on the disk.*

## CHAPTER 9

# Computer Programming

## WHAT IS A PROGRAM?

A computer needs a set of instructions telling it every single step that it must take to complete any job. Unlike other machines, a computer stores this set of instructions within its internal storage and the set of instructions is called a *program*. The people who write the sets of instructions have to work out all the steps that need to be taken to complete a job, and then write them down in the correct logical sequence. They are called *computer programmers*. They also have to test the programs to make sure that the computer will do the job properly before it works on real data.

## INSTRUCTIONS

Each instruction in a computer program has two parts:

1. An *operation code*, which tells the computer what to do with the data.
2. An *address*, or some addresses, which tells the computer where the data on which the operation is to be carried out can be found *or* contains the data itself.

Suppose a computer uses the letter A as the operation code for an add instruction. This is a simple example. In real life, operation codes are more difficult binary codes, but never mind. Suppose also, that each address in the instruction is three numbers long. The instruction:

A 100 200

means add the data at address 100 to the data at address 200, not, as you might think, add 100 to 200 giving the result 300. The computer's control unit must go to address 100, find the data there, and move it into a register in the arithmetic and logic unit (ALU). It must then go to address 200 and do the same with the data there. It then adds the data together, and moves the result back into one of the storage addresses, either 100 or 200, depending on how that particular computer works.

Say this computer puts the result into the second address, and before the instruction was carried out this was the data in the addresses:

| Address 100 | Address 200 |
|---|---|
| 3 0 4 2 | 0 1 4 3 |

After the instruction the data in the addresses would look like this:

| Address 100 | Address 200 |
|---|---|
| 3 0 4 2 | 3 1 8 5 |

The result of the add is in address 200. The data at address 100 remains as it was, because when it was read into the ALU it was not removed, as we saw in Chapter 6.

As we have seen, a computer program is a set of instructions, sometimes thousands of instructions, all written in the correct sequence, to be worked through one at a time by the computer's control unit.

## TYPES OF INSTRUCTION

The computer needs different types of instruction as listed below.

### *1. Input/output instructions*

These instructions read data into internal storage from input devices or external storage devices. They write data and information out from internal storage onto output devices, such as printers, or onto external storage devices. Input instructions have an operation code and the address in internal storage for the data to be put into. Output instructions have an operation code and either the address of the data to be written out from internal storage or the data item itself.

### *2. Arithmetic instructions*

A computer that could not do arithmetic would not be of much use. Computers can be programmed to do very complex calculations, even though they do them by repeating simple addition sums over and over again. All computer programming languages allow programmers to add; many subtract, multiply, divide, and raise numbers to powers, like $6^3$, or $6 \times 6 \times 6$. Arithmetic instructions have an operation code and either the address (or addresses) of the data on which the operation is to be carried out, or the data item itself.

### *3. Data manipulation instructions*

In many computer programs there is a great deal of simple moving around of data. For example, data items often need to be stored somewhere in internal storage to be looked at later. Data needs to be moved from input addresses to processing addresses, or from processing addresses to output addresses. Sometimes the data needs to be changed, or edited, as it is moved. For example, an amount to be printed out on a cheque may need a '£' sign put in front of it, and * put between the £ sign and the first digit of the amount, like this £***23.13.

Programming languages need instructions that enable programmers to move data from one storage address to another, move instructions, and edit instructions.

### *4. Jump instructions*

What gives a computer the power to carry out complicated tasks is its ability to make decisions and jump to different places within the program according to those decisions.

There are two types of jump instruction. The first type is a *conditional* jump instruction. The computer can be instructed to look at data addresses and jump according to what it finds there. For example, it can compare two addresses, and jump to one instruction if the first address contains an item that is greater than that at the second address.

It can look at the contents of an address and jump to different instructions according to the contents. A personnel record might contain a data item that has a code to say whether the worker is single, married, divorced, or widowed, and the program might have to follow a different set of instructions according to the code. A conditional jump will cause the program to go to the correct set of instructions according to the code.

The other type of jump instruction is an *unconditional* jump, in most languages a GO TO instruction. This causes the program to go immediately to a different set of instructions, usually back to repeat a set of instructions over again. A set of instructions that is repeated within a program is called a *loop*.

Jump instructions are slightly different from other types of instruction because, although they have an operation code and an address, this address is not an address of data but the address of the instruction that the program should now jump to.

*Now work on Assignments 33 and 34 in the* Teacher's Manual.

Jump instruction

## A SIMPLE PROGRAM

Now let us look at a very simple program to see examples of the types of instruction. Say we wanted to write a computer program to add numbers together and print out the total of the numbers. The person using the program enters the numbers one at a time, and when they have been entered, 0 is entered to show that the program should now print the total.

## FLOWCHARTS

Programmers use what are known as *flowcharts* to show the logical steps to be taken by a program. A flowchart is a logic diagram which uses the symbols shown on the next page.

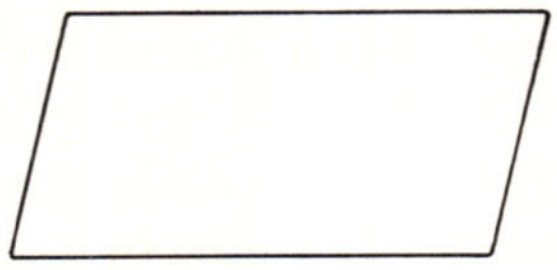

to mean an input/output instruction

to mean a processing step

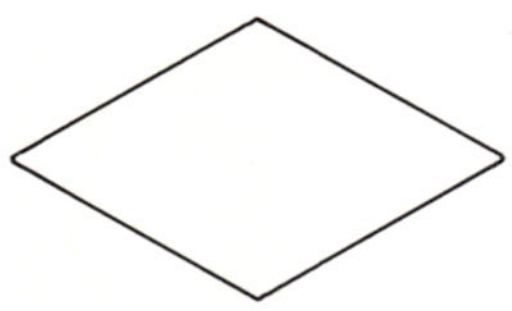

to mean a place in the program where a decision is made, which will mean a conditional jump

to mean a place where the program starts or finishes

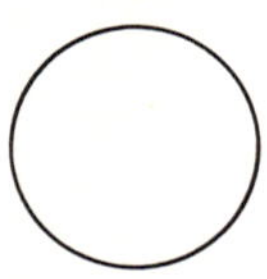

to mean an off page connector if the program is too large for the flowchart to be drawn on one page.

The symbols are connected by flowlines, with arrows to show the way the processing flows, like this: ——▶.

The flowchart for our simple little program looks like Fig. 9.1. See if you

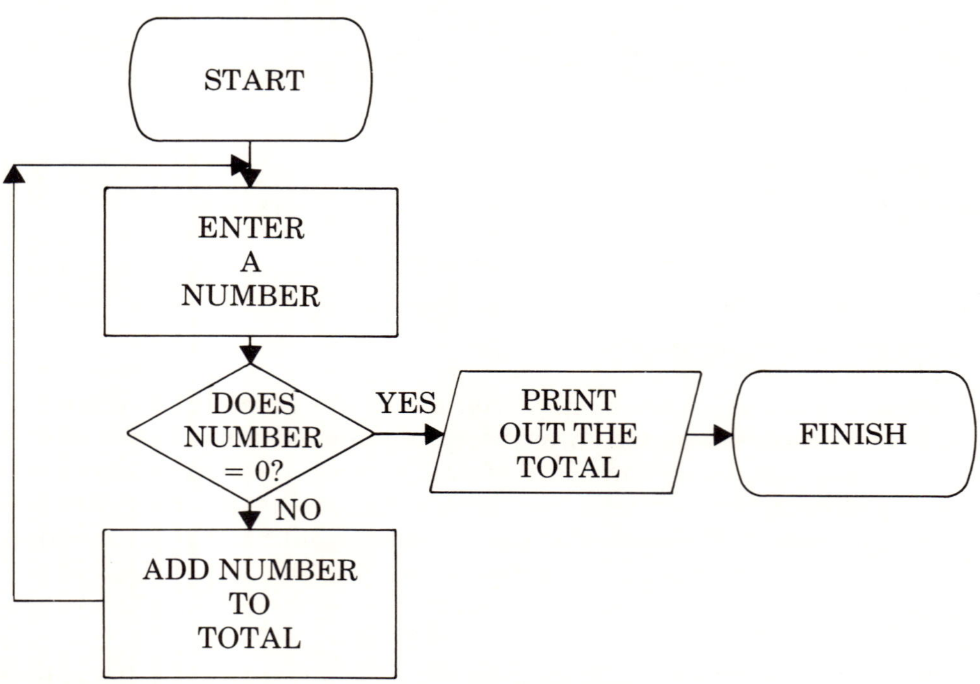


**Figure 9.1** *Flowchart*

can follow the diagram. Notice that the words in each symbol explain what is happening. Many people draw flowcharts, and instead of writing a description of what is happening in English they write the actual computer program instructions. This is silly. A flowchart should help a person who is trying to find out how the program works. A stranger to the program will not be helped by a flowchart that simply lists the instructions in the program over again.

*Now work on Assignment 35 in the* Teacher's Manual.

## A BASIC PROGRAM EXPLAINED

Some of you may already be familiar with a programming language called BASIC. It is the language that is used on home computers, and the language with which many computer users first come into contact. You may well have done some programming in BASIC at school. Our simple program written in BASIC looks like this:

```
10 LET A = 0 (set an accumulator to zero)
20 INPUT R (read in a number)
30 IF R = 0 THEN 60 (does number = 0)
40 LET A = A + R (add number to the accumulator)
50 GO TO 20 (loop back to repeat)
60 PRINT A (print the contents of the accumulator)
70 END
```

You can compare this with the flowchart.

BASIC is a readily understandable programming language. It is what is known as an *interactive* language. In simple terms this means that programs written in BASIC can request the user to intervene at various stages in the running of the program either to enter data or take decisions that will affect the operation of the program. The instructions, at this level, are very near to our own language. Let us look at an instruction and see what each part of it means.

```
10 LET A = 0
```

The 10 is the line number of the instruction. You will see that I have left 10 between each line number in the program. This is because we might, at a later time, want to add more instructions to the program. The line number determines the sequence in which the instructions are carried out, and so we need to leave room between each instruction for the addition of new instructions. The ability to add new instructions anywhere in a program makes BASIC an ideal language for developing and testing programs at a VDU terminal. The 10 is also the *address* of this instruction. More about this in a moment.

LET is the operation code for the instruction. We use this operation code for all data manipulation and arithmetic instructions in BASIC.

A is an address where we will store data. It is not a computer address in internal storage, but what is known as a *symbolic* address. You will see that we refer to the address A also in the instructions at line 40 and line 60 in the program. It is important that you remember that A is an address. I will explain symbolic address a bit more in a minute.

The = 0 part of the instruction simply means the contents of address A become equal to zero.

*Now work on Assignment 36 in the* Teacher's Manual.

## PROGRAM TRANSLATION

You can see that the instructions in our BASIC program all have an operation code and an address or addresses. The computer cannot, however, use this program written in BASIC. The programs that are stored, and that work, within a computer have to be in machine language. The BASIC program must be *translated* into the *machine language* before the program is used, or as the program is being used. The computer's control unit expects an instruction to have an operation code that matches the operation codes that it can understand. These codes are usually complicated binary codes. It also expects the addresses of data to be in binary code, as we saw in Chapter 6.

## MACHINE LANGUAGE

In the early days of computing all programs were written in machine language. Writing in machine language is a complex job. The programmer has to remember what the binary machine codes are. He or she also has to remember where data is stored within the memory addresses of the machine, and where instructions are located within memory for jump instructions.

Over the years the number of operation codes that a computer has to choose from has grown. The size of memory has also grown. A person writing programs in machine language these days has much more to remember. Machine language programming calls for rare and special skills.

## SYMBOLIC PROGRAMMING LANGUAGES

As the use of computers has grown, so businesses have needed more and more programmers. The supply of people capable of programming in machine language is limited, and so the makers of computers have had to find a way of making their machines easier to program. They would not have been able to sell them otherwise. They therefore introduced *symbolic* programming languages. These languages replace the machine operation codes by codes that are easy to remember. Computer people call them *mnemonic* operation codes, which means easy to remember. For example, the operation code A might mean add, S, subtract, M, move, and so on. Some programming languages even use the actual English words as operation codes, add, subtract, move, and so on. The programmer can remember mnemonic operation codes more easily than machine codes. Instead of machine addresses, symbolic programming languages use symbolic addresses, sometimes known as *labels*. In our simple BASIC program we used the letter A as the symbolic address, or label, of the address in memory where we wanted to accumulate the total. We used the letter R as the symbolic address, or label, of the address in memory where we wanted to input data. You can perhaps now see why I called A an address. Sensible programmers will also use symbolic addresses that are easy to remember so that they can easily think of the symbolic address of a data item as they are writing the program. I used the symbolic address A because A is the first letter of 'accumulator'. and A is where I accumulate the total I want to print.

There are two types of symbolic programming languages, *low level* and *high level*.

### *Low level languages*

Low level languages are not very different from machine languages. They use mnemonic operation codes and symbolic addresses, but the instructions are written like the instructions in machine language, an operation code followed by one or two addresses. A coding sheet for writing a low level language program might look something like Fig. 9.2.

| LABEL | OP. CODE | ADDRESS A | ADDRESS B | COMMENT |
|---|---|---|---|---|
| | | | | |

**Figure 9.2** *Coding sheet*

Because low level languages are like machine languages they are often referred to as being *machine oriented*, or leaning towards a machine. Different types of computer have their own low level language, which means that if a business writes all its programs in the low level language for the computer it uses and then gets a different type of computer it will have to rewrite all its programs in the low level language for the new computer.

Furthermore, because low level languages are like machine languages in the way they are written, programming in them still calls for a great deal of skill, which limits the number of people available to program in them.

### *High level languages*

High level languages are not machine oriented, they are *user oriented.* They have been developed to make computer programming a job that many more people can do, even people who are not computer specialists but do other jobs, like scientists, engineers, or accountants. Indeed, some high level languages have been developed for particular users. FORTRAN, for example, which stands for FORmula TRANslation, enables scientists, engineers, and other such users to write programs easily to handle mathematical formulae. COBOL, which stands for COmmon Business Oriented Language is specially designed for business use. BASIC is ideal for writing and developing programs at a VDU terminal, essential for the home microcomputer user.

High level languages are not designed for a particular machine. They are *universal.* A program written in a high level language can be taken from one type of machine and used, with perhaps some minor changes, on another. If a business writes all its programs in COBOL and then buys a different type of computer it will not have to rewrite all its programs for the new machine.

Programming in high level languages is much easier than in low level. High level languages are designed to make programming an easier and non-specialist job. COBOL, for example, is really not that different from English, and can be learnt relatively quickly. Nearly all computer programs are now written in symbolic programming languages, and most in high level languages. We have seen, however, that the computer can only understand and use programs written in machine language.

## WHAT HAPPENS IN PROGRAM TRANSLATION

In program translation we get the computer to *translate* the programs from symbolic language to machine language. The people who have developed

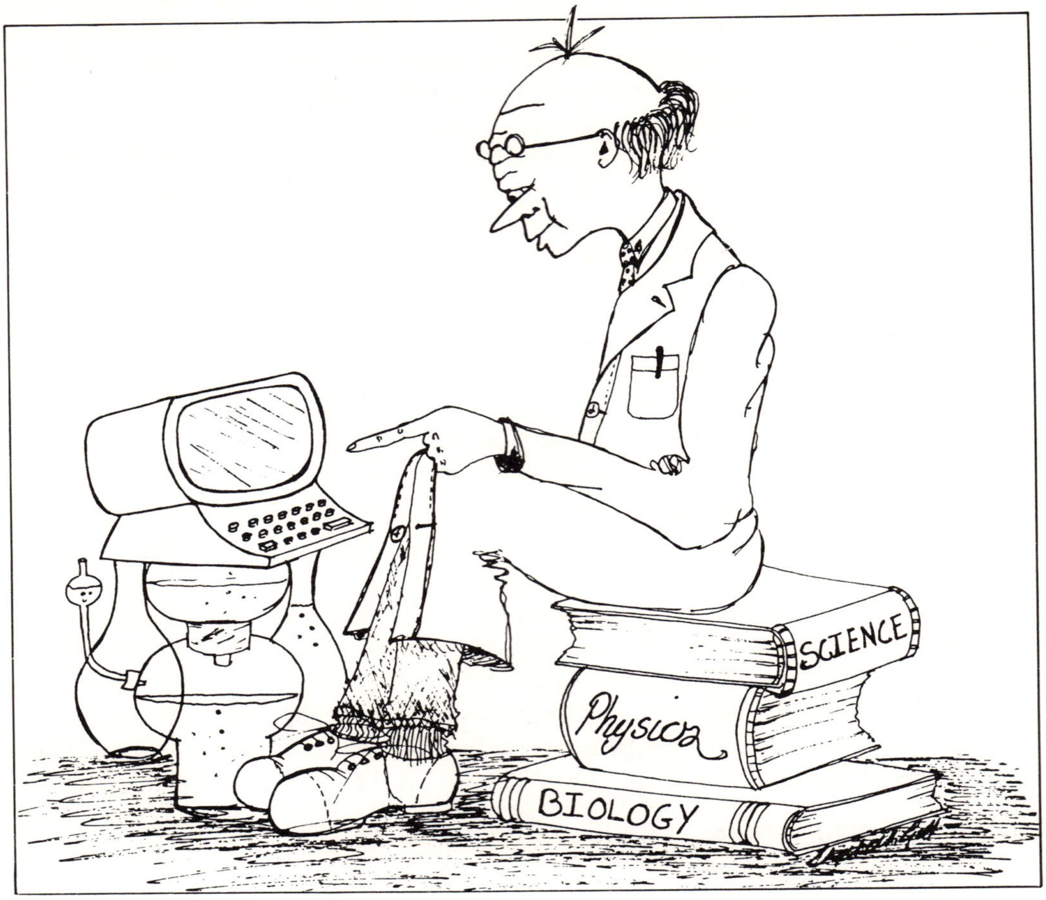


Scientist in a white coat using a computer

the symbolic languages have written special computer programs to do the translation. These programs change the mnemonic operation codes of the symbolic language to machine operation codes. They change symbolic addresses, or labels, into machine addresses. They also find what errors they can in the symbolic program and inform the programmer about them. The programmer may have used a wrong operation code or wrong addresses and the translator program will be able to point that out to the programmer. The errors found by the translator are called *diagnostics*.

There are two other words you should also know. The symbolic program, before it is translated, is known as a *source program*. The machine language after translation is known as an *object program*.

## ASSEMBLERS

The programs that translate low level programs into machine language are called *assemblers*. Indeed, low level languages are often called *assembler* languages. Because low level languages are written like machine languages, assemblers have a fairly simple task to do. The instructions in the low level language are converted one at a time into machine language. Usually each instruction in the source program is translated into some machine language instruction. Because of this, computer people call low level language instructions *micro instructions*.

## COMPILERS

The programs that translate high level languages into machine languages are called *compilers*. Compilers have a more difficult job to do. Instructions in a high level language program are not at all like machine language instructions. The compiler often has to translate one instruction in the source program into many instructions in the object program. Because of this, computer people call high level language instructions *macro instructions*. To add to the compiler's problems there are fewer rules about the way high level programs should be written compared to the strict rule of low level languages. All in all, compilers are very clever programs.

## INTERPRETERS

There are some high level languages that are translated by another type of translator program. This program is known as an *interpreter*. On most microcomputers there is a BASIC language interpreter in the ROM memory of the machine which is available the moment the machine is turned on. Many BASIC programs are interpreted rather than compiled.

### *How an interpreter works*

An interpreter is different from an assembler or a compiler. Instead of translating the symbolic source program into a machine language object program, it looks at each instruction in the source program and translates it to machine language just before it carries out the instruction as the program is being run. This means that if there are loops in the program, where instructions need to be carried out over and over again, those instructions are translated over and over again. Such programs will, therefore, take longer to run than similar programs that have been translated once only by an assembler or a compiler.

### *Why use interpreters?*

You may well wonder why we bother with interpreters then. Why not compile a BASIC program so that it will take less time to run? In fact, interpreters are very useful. They enable us to write programs at a VDU terminal, try them out, alter them, and try out the alterations until we have a good, working program. We may well then, of course, compile that working program so that it runs more quickly, but the interpreter is an ideal tool for program development. For languages where we do not have an interpreter we have to write the program, compile it, try it out, alter the symbolic source program, compile it again, try it out again, and so on. As compiling a program can take some time you can perhaps see the value of our interpreter. You may have already seen how you can write and test a BASIC program on a microcomputer for yourselves.

## PROGRAM TESTING

Once a program has been translated into machine language, and all the diagnostics have been sorted out, the programmer will then test the program to see if it works. To do this he or she runs special data through the program to see if it is processed by the computer the way it should be. If it does not the programmer will have to find out what is wrong with the program, put it right, and then test it again. This process continues until the programmer is sure that the program has no faults. Finding the faults in a computer program is called *debugging* the program.

The number of programming languages available to computer users grows and grows, and the way that programs are written has changed over the years. Some say that the computer programmer within businesses will disappear in the future, and that people will buy their programs with their computers. We will consider this again in Chapter 10.

*Now work on Assignments 37, 38, 39 and 40 in the* Teacher's Manual, *and on Programs J, I and H on the disk.*

CHAPTER 10

# Computer Networks and Operating Systems

## NETWORKS

In this chapter we will be looking at two subjects, but I hope that you will be able to see at the end of it why I have talked about the two in the same chapter.

## LOCAL AREA NETWORKS

A computer *network* is a collection of computer hardware connected together. Some might think that this is an over simplification, but for now we can think of it like that.

You may well have seen a computer network in your own college or school. It may be nothing more than a room full of microcomputers all linked to a controlling microcomputer. The controlling micro will typically be more sophisticated than the others, and will probably have a hard disk. The other micros will use the hard disk through the controlling micro. This means that all users can put files of data and software onto the hard disk. It means that users can get at the software and files of other users, if they are allowed to, so data and programs can be shared around the network. It may even be possible for the other micros to 'borrow' power from the bigger controlling micro if they want to tackle a job that is too big for them to handle by themselves. The computers and other devices in a small network like this will be linked together by ordinary coaxial cable, the sort of cable that is used for television aerials. There will be no need to rent telephones or other external links for the network. Networks like this are called *local area networks*.

## WIDE AREA NETWORKS

Simple types of network are the basis for the large and complex computer networks that we see nowadays. Some large organizations have vast networks. They have many computers of different shapes and sizes linked together. There is an enormous range of other hardware within the network, input devices, output devices, and storage devices. The computers and other peripheral devices are often many miles apart, sometimes even thousands of miles. Communication satellites these days enable people to talk to computers on the other side of the world.

In such networks, where the hardware is spread over vast distances, the computers and peripheral devices are linked together by miles of telephone and other links which are provided by the Post Office. These links connect input and output devices together, input and output devices to computers, and computers to other computers within the network. There are so many links going in different directions that if you could look at such networks from above and see all the links laid out it would often look like a fishing net. You can see why they are called networks. (I have heard it said that they are called networks because the claims about them are often fishy.) These large networks, with hardware spread over great distances, are called *wide area networks*.

### *Use of wide area networks*

Wide area networks are very common these days. You will be able to think of organizations that use them for yourselves, but I will give you some examples.

### *Banks*

Probably the banks are the best examples of organizations that use large computer networks. Their computer centres at different places over the country are linked by telephone and other land lines to each other and to all their branches. They control things like cashpoints and enable staff within branches to find information about customers' accounts from the files at the computer centres. Data about customers' transactions are sent from branches to the computers through the network along the links at the end of each day's trading so that the customers' accounts are kept much more up to date than they were before computers.

### *Travel businesses*

There are excellent examples in the travel business. Airlines use networks to link their offices, airports, and computer centres throughout the country. The computer files keep information about flights and bookings so that any sales office can give really up-to-date information about seats available. The sales offices can book seats through the network and have tickets printed out there and then by the computer. Some airlines also allow travel agents to use the network so that they can find out about flights from their offices. Not only that, the airlines also keep other information besides flight details in their computer files. They keep information about hotels, theatres, and other places that may be of use or interest to a traveller. They can make bookings for these places as well through the networks. Their networks crisscross the world so that bookings can be made in other countries.

## DISTRIBUTED SYSTEMS

Most large organizations have a computer network of some sort. Networks have enabled them to arrange their computing power in new ways. For example, instead of using the services of one, large, mainframe central computer, businesses can now have a variety of different computers spread around the business, all linked together and to the central computer. This can be better than the old arrangement. It means that staff at different places within the business can have control over the writing and running of their own computer systems instead of having to rely on a central office to do it. Often the computer staff at a central office were out of touch with problems at other places within the business. This made it difficult to design good systems for them.

Now it is possible for offices to obtain their own computer, a mini or micro perhaps, and design their own systems. At the same time they can send their data to the central computer files through the network for the overall management of the business. They can get information back from the central computer files for their systems through the network. Networks that are arranged in this way are often called *distributed systems*.

Networks also enable managers at offices throughout the business to obtain information from the central computer's files, even though they may be at offices that are many miles from the computer.

## VIEWDATA SERVICES

Another important example of large computer networks is *viewdata* services. A viewdata service allows members of the public to have, at a price, access to information kept in computer files. Examples of viewdata services in Britain are PRESTEL, run by the post office, and TELETEXT.

Subscribers to a viewdata service access the computer files through their telephones and see the results of their enquiries on their television screens, which are then really VDU terminals for the computer network. Each time they make an enquiry for some information they are charged for it.

At the other end of the service, people who want to sell information buy space in the computer files. They can then enter their information and keep it up to date. Each time somebody looks at the information, part of the charge is passed on to the people who provided it.

## HOME SHOPPING

You may have seen PRESTEL or TELETEXT yourselves, so you will know what sort of information it can provide. Weather forecasts, travel timetables, and radio and television schedules are some examples. In the future, viewdata services will become much more important than providers of information. People will be able to do their shopping from their own homes. The viewdata service will show on television screens lists of goods with prices from local shops. Shoppers will be able to select goods by pressing keys on a keypad connected to the network. The shop will be informed of the order and will deliver the goods to the customer later. Not only that, eventually the shop will also be able to transfer the payment for the goods from the customer's bank account to the shop's bank account through the same viewdata network automatically.

Shopping at home

Viewdata services are likely to have a major effect on our lives. I can see a time when we become dependent upon them for all our information needs. The television screen could even replace books, magazines, and newspapers.

*Now work on Assignment 41 in the* Teacher's Manual.

## MULTIACCESS

The use of networks has also meant changes in the way that computers work. In the early days of computing when organizations had a computer centre, that was the only place where the computer was used. Programs were run on the computer one after another under the control of a human operator. The only people who could get at the computer were the staff of the computer centre.

When computers started to be linked to telephone lines so that people at other places could run programs or ask for information from the computer, things had to change. Computers now need to allow more than one program to be running at one time. They need to allow other people to have use of the computer when it is already being used. This is known as *multiaccess*.

## SECURITY PROBLEMS

The use of networks to allow people from different places to use the computer through VDUs and other devices means that there are problems. People can get at a VDU and break into the computer systems. They can look at data that they should not look at. They can steal programs or information. They can spoil computer files. You may have seen programmes about this on television, and so will already know that this can happen. Even the owners of home computers can buy a device called a *modem*, which allows them to link their computer to the telephone system. The input and output devices of business networks also use modems as connections to their telephone links. If they are clever, outsiders can find out how to break into computer networks and do considerable damage to them. People who do this sort of thing are called *hackers*.

## OPERATING SYSTEMS

A human operator cannot deal with the problems of multiaccess. It would always be necessary to be answering the telephone and loading new systems into the computer for the different users. It would also be impossible to deal with the problem of stopping unauthorized people from breaking into computer systems and stealing from them or damaging them. A human operator is also liable to make mistakes when using the computer. That is the trouble with humans. Unfortunately, on a computer some mistakes can be disastrous. In the early days of computing one of the most common mistakes made was loading the wrong master files onto a storage device. This often caused the data on those files to be lost. You can imagine just how much of a disaster losing a system's master files can be.

Some way had to be found to get over these problems. The answer was to write computer programs that would take care of them. These programs are very complex and are called *operating systems*. As soon as a computer is turned on, an operating system takes over the running of the computer.

The operating system receives commands from users of the computer and makes sure that they are obeyed. In fact, what really happens is that the computer, through the operating system, ends up controlling the human operator.

Computer controlling the operator

### *The tasks of operating systems*

Let us look at some of the things an operating system does for a large computer system where there are many users at different places, as there will be on a network. It constantly looks at all the terminals attached to the system to see if anybody wants to use the computer. If there are, it makes sure that that person is authorized to use the system. Authorized users will have user codes and passwords for the operating system to check. It will turn away unauthorized people and probably report that they tried to break into the system.

For authorized users, the operating system looks at what they want to do. They will almost certainly want to run a program of some sort. The operating system sees if that can be done right away. The computer may already be full of programs, so this user will have to queue for a while.

When the operating system decides that the user's program can be run, it makes all the arrangements for it to be run. This may mean telling the human operator to load things onto storage devices, input devices, or output devices. It will mean loading the actual program into memory from a storage device.

When the program is loaded into the computer's memory it may be one of several programs being run at the same time. The operating system makes sure that all the programs in turn are given some processing time by the processing unit.

We have already seen that the operating system will tell the human operator to load the correct storage device so that the user will have the files that he or she needs for his or her program on-line. The operating system will also make sure that the correct storage devices were loaded by looking at identifying labels at the front of the files. At the same time, it will make sure that the files can be shown to this user. That information will also be in the file labels.

In addition to all these jobs, operating systems also make sure that files are copied for security purposes. They provide input and output instructions for the transfer of data between memory and peripheral devices to be included in users' programs.

There are other jobs that operating systems do, but discussion of them is beyond the scope of this book. You now at least have some idea of what an important piece of software an operating system is. I hope that you can also see why I have included operating systems in the chapter with networks. The jobs that are done by the operating system are needed for a computer network to work properly.

If you have used a microcomputer you will have used an operating system. Although it will not have done all the jobs of a large system operating system, it will have done some of them. For example, it will have looked after your files for you and made sure that others could not get at your files unless you allowed it. You may be able to think of other jobs it did for you.

*Now work on Assignment 42 (and 7 for revision) in the* Teacher's Manual.

CHAPTER 11

# Computers and Society

## THE EFFECTS OF COMPUTERS

The last thing I would like to do in this book is take a personal look at how computers may have changed our lives so far, and what effects they may have in the future.

We must all be affected by computers in some way. Their usage has spread so much since the 1960s that, even if we do not realize it, computers must play a part somewhere in our lives. There are few organizations, large or small, that do not use a computer for record keeping. Your name must appear on a computer file somewhere. It may be at your local area health authority headquarters, your education authority office, your library, perhaps even your school or college.

## COMPUTERS AND SHOPPING

Many large stores now depend upon computers to control their cash registers and stocks of goods. This, too, will affect you. Computers are used by banks, building societies, insurance companies, and other such institutions. Again, if you use their services you will be, indirectly, affected by their computers.

The way that you are affected may be varied and uncertain. We have already seen that computers are such powerful tools that businesses should be using them to our advantage. Shops and offices should be using them to improve the service they give to us. Shops, for example, should be using computers to keep track of what people buy so that they can provide the goods we require. The stocks of goods available to us should therefore be better. Other aspects of shopping should have improved at the same time. Computer controlled checkouts should enable us to get out of shops more quickly, should reduce queues at tills, and should even give us better receipts for our goods.

Unfortunately, it does not always work like that. The use of computers often causes a loss of flexibility. The computer demands that things are done in a certain way, therefore the shop is often run to suit the computer rather than the customer. Many large stores, for example, use bar-code readers or other such devices at checkouts. It is to their advantage. There is no longer any need for goods to be priced on shelves. The shop can therefore save staff.

Many customers, however, do not like this new style of shopping. They like to have prices on goods. They like to be able to check them as they are cashed up at a checkout. When prices are only put on shelves, and not on individual packets, this is not possible. Some people, particularly those from older generations, are suspicious of the new equipment. They may well avoid shops that use such methods.

Shops that are dependent upon computers to control the checkout points need computer systems that are completely reliable. If the computer breaks down, then the checkouts cannot work and chaos is caused within the stores.

In some groups of stores, computers have taken over stocking of shops completely. Computers calculate how many of each item of stock should go to each store. The sales assistants within the stores never know what is going to be delivered. They cannot ask for extra stocks of items that sell well. They cannot let customers know if stocks of an item will be received or order items for customers. Very often it appears that the shops are being run by the computer, and that the service provided is not designed to help the customer.

## COMPUTERS AND BANKS

Banks now use computers extensively. Customers' accounts are kept on computer files. The computers print out customer statements, look after cashpoints, and do many other of the banks' jobs from computer centres throughout the country. There is no doubt that banks have benefited greatly from the use of computers.

Again, however, there are those who would say that the use of computers has done little for the service that banks provide for their customers. For example, once upon a time each customer of a bank was dealt with by the branch of the bank where their account was kept. A customer could stroll into his home bank at any time and ask for a bank statement and be given one immediately. Now he has to wait for the computer to produce one and send it to him a few days later.

One of the major new developments in banking in recent years has been the introduction of cashpoints. There is no doubt that this has been a big step in customer service, a step that would have been impossible without computers. However, there are people who will not use cashpoints. Cashpoints will let customers draw out money or see what is in their accounts at any time, but some people do not like using such machines, and do not trust them. You might well say that that is okay. People who do not want to use cashpoints can draw money inside the bank in the normal way. Fine, but there are dangers that we need to look out for. Paying money out by computer through a cashpoint is cheaper than paying it out over a counter inside a bank. For this reason, banks would very much like to see more and more people using cashpoints. What if they decide that because of cashpoints, banks do not need to open for as long as they do now? What if they decide that they can close some branches, perhaps in less well populated areas, and replace them with cashpoints?

Should we be wary when the computer dictates the service that is provided and, instead of improving the service, reduces it? Some banks, for example, now let the computer decide when a customer should have a new cheque book. There is almost an attitude of the computer knowing best, yet how will the computer know when a customer is going on holiday and needs extra cheques? How will the computer know when a customer is going to receive a lot of unexpected bills?

## DEPENDENCY ON COMPUTERS

It is difficult to tell how much computers will enter our lives in the future. I forsee a future where we will depend upon them for much of our everyday lives. We will be able to shop through them and receive day-to-day informa-

Shopping by Computer

tion through them. We can already see evidence of this in PRESTEL, viewdata, and other such services we receive through our televisions. Already we can pay bills through them from our homes. They may replace newspapers, magazines, and even books. We will be able to call up the information we need through computers to be displayed in our living rooms. We may well have a national computer network that every home will be connected to, just like the electricity grid network we now take for granted.

What will this mean for our lifestyles. It may well mean better services, cheaper goods, more free time to enjoy ourselves. It may also mean less service, more rigid standards for us to meet, less choice, less personal contact with others, and more unemployment. We may become so dependent upon the computer that we have to consult it for everything we do.

I think it is important that we think about these things. As more and more organizations become dependent upon the computer, we need to be sure that they do not use it as an excuse to reduce the service we receive. We are told too often these days that we cannot do something because the computer will not allow it, or that something has gone wrong because of the computer. Computers can only do what humans let them do.

## THREATS TO PRIVACY

Another aspect of the spreading use of computers is the threat they make to our personal privacy. Some say that this threat is overstated. They say that data is easier to get at when it is kept in old-fashioned manual files. Data kept on computer files is safer because you cannot read data from

Somebody looking into a filing cabinet

reels of magnetic tape or from magnetic disks. Before a person can find out what is on a computer file he needs to be a computer expert. Data written on bits of paper in manual files can easily be read by anybody.

Others, however, are not so sure. There are other dangers to privacy through the use of computer files. We have already seen that one of the main advantages of computer files is that a great deal of data can be stored in a very small space, and that the data can quickly and easily be found and displayed. A problem with computer files is that because of this there will be a temptation for organizations to collect lots of data on people, more than is really needed. It is easy for one organization to pass data to another organization through their computer networks. A bank, for example, may pass on information about a customer from its computer files to a shop's computer files. This is very worrying. People will not know what data is kept on them by organizations. They may give information to one organization that they would not like another to have. Mistakes may be made as data passes from one place to another so that the records kept on a person are inaccurate.

Let me give you an example. Suppose someone buys a music centre on credit from a shop. Later on he fails to make a payment on the music centre because his bank makes a mistake with his bank account. The shop's computer files make a note that he has fallen behind with his payments, and that information is passed on to another computer file that shops use to see if a customer is creditworthy.

The purchaser may go to the shop to explain that his bank has made a mistake. The shop may accept his explanation and put its computer files right. What, though, if it does not pass on that information to the other computer file? The purchaser may find that, in the future, he cannot get any credit, and he will not know why.

## MISUSE OF DATA FILES

The passing around of data between computer systems is an easy thing to do. We already know that some businesses sell their computer files of customers' names and addresses to others. This is why people receive advertising brochures through the post. It has also been shown that it is not too difficult to get at data stored in computer files. Computer files containing personal data that are linked to a large computer network are available to anybody who can get onto a VDU terminal attached to the network, unless the files are protected properly (see Chapter 10). Not only that, home computer owners have shown that they can get at the files of computer networks. By buying a simple and cheap modem (see Chapter 10) they can link into computer networks through their telephones.

## PRIVACY LEGISLATION

The problem of the privacy of data kept on computer files has so concerned the government that a Data Protection Act has now been passed. This attempts to give some control over personal data kept on computer files. It means that in the future people who keep such data must register the fact that they do so with a data protection body. They must say what data will be kept and what it will be used for. They must say if any of the data will be passed on to others. They must show how the data is protected from prying eyes or hackers. And what is even more important, they must allow people to see the data that is kept on them and to put right any mistakes in that data. The man in our music centre example would be able to find out why he was not allowed credit and be able to put the matter right. It is to be hoped that in the future those setting up files of personal data will think about the data they need and about its protection.

In this book we have examined the computer, a wonderful tool that has changed many things over the last 25 years. I leave you to decide whether it is for good or bad. What I do hope is that you will now be able to see that the computer is nothing more than a tool. We should use it as such and not let the computer use us. It should be used to improve our lives, not spoil them.

*Now work on Assignments 43 and 44 in the* Teacher's Manual.